C. Knapp

KINGS OF JUDAH

C. Knapp

KINGS OF JUDAH

Originally Published, 1909
Revised, 2004

Originally published as part
of a combined volume:
Kings of Judah and Israel

ISBN: 1-59387-008-6

Copyright © 2004 ECS Ministries

All rights reserved. No part of this book may be reproduced or transmitted in any form or by any means, electronic or mechanical, including photocopying and recording, or by any information storage and retrieval system including the World Wide Web, without the prior written permission from the Publisher. Permission is not needed for brief quotations embodied in critical articles or reviews.

Unless otherwise indicated, Scripture quotations in this book are from the King James Version of the Bible.

Scripture quotations indicated N.TR. are from John Nelson Darby's translation of the Old Testament.

Printed in the United States of America
2004

CONTENTS

The Reigns of Saul, David, and Solomon: An Introduction by H. A. Ironside	7
Author's Introduction	17
Chronological Table	27
Rehoboam	29
Abijah	37
Asa	43
Jehoshaphat	53
Jehoram	65
Ahaziah	71
Jehoash	75
Amaziah	87
Uzziah	95
Jotham	103
Ahaz	107
Hezekiah	117
Manasseh	139
Amon	147
Josiah	151
Jehoahaz	163
Jehoiakim	167
Jehoiachin	173
Zedekiah	179
Bibliography	185

THE REIGNS OF SAUL, DAVID AND SOLOMON: AN INTRODUCTION BY H. A. IRONSIDE

In complying with the request of the author for an introduction to his truly practical commentary on the books of Kings and Chronicles, I shall attempt to briefly summarize the histories of the three kings of the undivided monarchy, and that only so far as they are set before us in Kings and Chronicles. The lives of Saul and David are much more fully revealed in the books of Samuel, but others have written at length on them as there portrayed, and their writings are still available.

Chronicles opens with the genealogies of the children of Israel, tracing the chosen race right back to Adam. With his name the record begins and, so far as nature is concerned, every name that follows is but another addition of the first man. "The second man is the Lord from heaven." For His coming the world was yet waiting. However, God was indeed quickening souls from the first. There can be no doubt that Adam had obtained divine life when he took God at His word. Accepting the declaration made to the serpent about the seed of the woman (Genesis 3:15), he called his wife's name Eve, "Living," believing that God had found a way to avert the terrible doom their sin had justly deserved. In believing that first gospel message Adam exercised faith; where there is faith, there is of necessity eternal life, and thus a new nature. In many of his offspring, therefore, the same blessed truth is present. And so through these lists, which God has seen fit to preserve and which will be forever kept on high, we see in some the fruit of the new life revealed to the glory of Him who gave it.

There is something intensely solemn in being permitted to go over such a record of names long forgotten by man, but every one of which God has remembered, with every detail of their pathway through this world. Some day our names likewise will be lost to mankind, but neither we nor our ways will be forgotten by God.

Esau's race, as well as that of Israel, is kept in mind; a race from which came mighty kings and princes before any king reigned over Israel (1 Chronicles 1:43). For "that was not first which is spiritual, but that which is natural; and afterward that which is spiritual" (1 Corinthians 15:46). Then, too, some in Israel are only remembered because of some fearful sin that was their ruin, and often the ruin of those associated with them. Those such as Er, and Achan the troubler of Israel (called here Achar), Reuben, who defiled his father's bed, and the heads of the half tribe of Manasseh, who "went a whoring after the gods of the people of the land."

On the other hand, it is sweet and edifying to the soul to notice the brief comments which, if this were a human book, would seem so out of place in the midst of long lists of names. What divine grace had been demonstrated as they trod their oftentimes lowly ways, with faith in exercise and the conscience active. Of this character is the lovely passage about Jabez, who was more honorable than his brethren because he set the Lord before him. His prayer tells of the longings of his soul: "Oh that thou wouldest bless me indeed, and enlarge my coast, and that thy hand might be with me, and that thou wouldest keep me from evil, that it may not grieve me!" We do not wonder when we read that "God granted him that which he requested" (1 Chronicles 4:9–10). The sons of Reuben and their allies who overcame the Hagarites are cited as another instance of the power of faith when "they cried to God in the battle, and He was entreated of them, because they put their trust in Him," (5:18–20). Nor does God forget Zelophehad, the man who had no sons to inherit after him, but who claimed a portion for his daughters, and learned that the strength of the Lord is made perfect in weakness (7:15).

There are precious lessons too of an illustrative nature that become evident as we patiently search this portion of the word of the Lord. Who can fail to see the lesson of "the potters, and those that dwelt among plants and hedges: there they dwelt with the king for his work" (4:23)? Surely this represents all who seek to care for the tender plants of the Lord's garden, as well as those who minister to hardier Christians that constitute the hedges. It is only as the servants dwell with the King that they are fit to carry on His work (4:23). The lesson of 1 Chronicles 9:26–34 is similar.

Saul's genealogy begins with 1 Chronicles 8:33, but his whole life is passed over in silence, and only his lamentable end recorded in chapter 10. He it was of whom God said, "I gave them a king in mine anger, and took him away in my wrath" (Hosea 13:11). It was a desire to be like the nations that led Israel to ask for a king; in giving them their request the Lord sent leanness into their souls. Saul was the man of the people's choice, but he was a dreadful disappointment. His dishonored death is on a par with his unhappy life, which is only hinted at in the closing verses of 1 Chronicles 10. All the sorrowful details have been left on record in the books bearing Samuel's name—the prophet who loved him so dearly, but who could not lead him in the ways of God. As another has well described Saul, he was "the man after the flesh." This tells the whole story. In all his life he seemed to have never truly been brought into the presence of God. His activities were all of the flesh, and his way of looking at things was only according to man, and the garish light of man's day. Defeated on Mount Gilboa, he finally committed suicide, and after his death became the laughingstock of the enemies of the Lord.

> So Saul died for his transgression which he committed against the LORD, even against the word of the LORD, which he kept not, and also for asking counsel of one that had a familiar spirit, to enquire of it; And enquired not of the LORD: therefore he slew him, and turned the kingdom unto David the son of Jesse (10:13–14).

Upon the fall of the people's choice, God's man appears on the scene. There is no mention here of the early experiences of David, except that the mighty men are those who went down to the rock to him when he was in the cave of Adullam, and others also who came to him when he was at Ziklag (1 Chronicles 12:1).

The account here given begins with the coming of all Israel to David at Hebron to make him king (1 Chronicles 11). The seven year reign over Judah is not mentioned. Acknowledged by the whole nation as God's appointed ruler, he begins at once the work of enlarging Israel's borders and delivering them from their enemies. Jebus, the fortress of the Jebusites, is taken and converted into the city of David, where he reigns in power, growing greater and greater, thus demonstrating the fact that the Lord of hosts was with him. The mighty men who had shared his rejection are now the sharers of his power and glory. It is a picture of the true David, God's beloved Son, who is yet to be presented in authority over all the earth. Then those who now cleave to Him in humility will be exalted with Him when He takes His great power and reigns.

The ark is brought up to the city of David, but only after the lesson has been learned that God will be sanctified in them that draw close to Him. We learn that, though Philistine carts may do for those who know not the mind of God, where His word is given it must be searched and obeyed. Great are the rejoicings of the people when the symbol of the covenant of the Lord is installed in the place prepared for it, and burnt sacrifices and peace offerings ascend in a cloud of fragrance to God (1 Chronicles 15–16). But when the king would build a house for the God of Israel, though encouraged by the prophet Nathan in his pious purpose, both king and prophet had to learn that the thoughts of God are above the thoughts of the best and most devoted men. Nathan has to inform him that it cannot be for him to build the house, because he has been a man of blood. When David's son is established in peace on the throne, he will build the house, and all will be in keeping with the times. David then is seen to picture the establishment of the kingdom through the destruction of the enemies of the Lord, while Solomon depicts the reign of peace that is to follow for the thousand years. Bowing in obedience to the word of the Lord, David begins to prepare for the work of the temple by gathering in abundance all the materials that he is able to obtain.

But it is made evident that the ideal King has not yet come. Before he resigns his crown to his son, failure is found in the man after God's own heart. His personal sin, which left so dreadful a blot on his character, is omitted in 1 Chronicles, as befits the character of the book. But his official failure in numbering the people is told in all faithfulness, as also the fact that it was Satan who provoked him to act as he did. But in amazing grace God overrules all to make David's sin the means of showing the site for the future temple of the Lord (1 Chronicles 21). Finally, having set all in order, and arranged even the courses of the priests and Levites who are to officiate in the glorious house of Jehovah, the aged monarch appointed Solomon, his son through Bathsheba, to be king in his stead. After solemnly instructing him both about the kingdom and the house that is to be built, "he died in a good old age, full of days, riches, and honour: and Solomon his son reigned in his stead" (29:28).

In the opening chapters of 1 Kings we see that his last days were not all bright. His failure to properly control his household brought him much sorrow, and embittered his cup when he was too feeble to exert himself as he would have desired. Adonijah's effort to secure the crown for himself resulted in disaster, and eventually in his own death, and Solomon's title is indisputably established.

Solomon's reign begins most auspiciously. He went to Gibeon, where the altar still remained with the tabernacle, to offer sacrifice. God appeared to him in the night with the wondrous message, "Ask what I shall give thee" (1 Kings 3:5). It was as though He placed all His resources at the disposal of faith. The young king prayed for wisdom and knowledge in order that he may care for the flock committed to him. It was a most remarkable prayer for one placed in his position, and the Lord displayed His pleasure by conferring on him exceeding abundantly above all that he asked or thought. His wisdom, celebrated to this day, was admired by his people and the surrounding nations wherever his fame was carried.

The main part of the chapters devoted to Solomon, in both Kings and Chronicles, is occupied with the account of the temple, every part of which was to depict the glory of the One greater than Solomon who was yet to come. The symbolism of this magnificent structure has been discussed at length by others, and would not properly belong in this introduction. At the dedication of the temple, which had gone up so silently, Jehovah entered in a manner that none might misunderstand, and took possession of the house as His own. Solomon's prayer on that occasion is prophetic of the sad history later recorded in these books. He seemed to see all that his people would yet have to pass through.

But light and gift are not sufficient of themselves to keep one in step with God. For a time all goes well with Solomon. His power is unprecedented. His fame is carried into all lands penetrated by the trader's caravan or touched by the ship of the voyager. The queen of Sheba comes from the uttermost parts of the earth to prove him with hard questions concerning the name of the Lord. She goes away with every question answered and her heart swelling with the glorious things that she has both seen and heard. The king's knowledge in all matters seems to be limitless. "And all the earth sought to Solomon, to hear his wisdom, which God had put into his heart" (1 Kings 10:24). It is sad that so glorious a record had to be blotted by the account of failure that the book of Kings records, but which is passed over in Chronicles.

"But King Solomon loved many strange women... when Solomon was old, his wives turned away his heart after other gods" (1 Kings 11:1,4). Such is the terrible fall of the man who was the most privileged of all the rulers that history, sacred or secular, records. He failed to keep his own heart. The Lord lost the place He had once had, and the result was that Solomon sinned grievously after all he had known and enjoyed of the things of God. Idolatry was established in the sight of the holy temple of the Lord. God was dishonored by the man who, above all, had received the most from Him. What a warning to everyone who has experienced His grace! May reader and writer lay it to heart!

As a result of Solomon's sins the Lord stirred up adversaries against him, and in the days of his son tore the kingdom from the house of David, with the exception of the two tribes. The rest of this book will consider this period more fully.

We would only add a few remarks to trace the roots of the division that took place at the death of Solomon. The kingdom was torn in two, never to be reunited until the day of Israel's regeneration still to come, when "the envy also of Ephraim shall depart...Ephraim shall not envy Judah, and Judah shall not vex Ephraim" (Isaiah 11:13).

As descendants of Joseph, who (in Jacob's and Moses' blessings) was exalted above and "separate from his brethren," Ephraim seems ever to have aspired to leadership in the nation. During the time of the Judges, Ephraim's pride had twice broken out in an arrogant manner. After the mighty victory of Gideon's little band over the Midianites that had invaded and ravaged the land, the men of Ephraim sharply criticized Gideon because he had not called them to the war—envying the fame of such a victory. Gideon's gracious answer to their boastful criticism averted a catastrophe (Judges 8:1–3). But their still more conceited rebuke of Jephthah on a later occasion brought upon Ephraim a terrible, though deserved, retribution (12:1–6).

When the Theocracy (God's direct rule in Israel) gave place to the kingdom by Israel's irreverent request, Saul, taken from "little Benjamin," is acclaimed by all Israel. Benjamin having been nearly annihilated for their sin some time before, and being Joseph's full brother, may for that reason have been more welcome to Ephraim. But when David, of the tribe of Judah, was revealed as God's anointed in the place of rejected Saul, and at Saul's death was made king in Hebron by Judah, he is not acclaimed. He was opposed by the other tribes, of whom Ephraim was chief, and a seven-year war followed. When the weak pretender of Saul's house (Ish-Bosheth) fell before the rising power of David and Judah, Israel is reunited in one kingdom under David's godly and righteous rule. The jealousy and strife that broke out on previous occasions is for the time forgotten and out of sight.

David's sin, and his son's wicked conduct, brought about upheavals in the kingdom. Later on, Solomon's departure from God and oppression of His people, caused them, at his death, to make demands on the new king Rehoboam. His insolent and foolish answer brings about the crisis in which the unthankful and heartless cry is heard, "What portion have we in David? neither have we inheritance in the son of Jesse: to your tents, O Israel! now see to thine own house, David" (1 Kings 12:16). Ephraim, headed by Jeroboam—an Ephraimite—then takes leadership of the ten tribes that had revolted from the house of David. Thereby a new kingdom is formed, in which every one in the line of their nineteen kings is an apostate from Jehovah.

I now leave the reader with what my beloved fellow servant has penned, praying that he may have your anointed eye and submissive heart, which alone makes the truth living and real in the soul.

AUTHOR'S INTRODUCTION

It is the author's purpose in this volume to review briefly the histories of the kings of Judah, as recorded in the inspired books of the Kings and Chronicles. These histories are given to us in more or less detail, and do not read exactly the same in each book. God has surely a purpose in this, and it is the glory of saints to search out these matters and to discover, if possible, why these differences exist. There can be no contradiction for "there is one Spirit," and He who inspired the historian of the Kings also controlled and directed the writer of the Chronicles.

These two historical books of the Old Testament bear a relation to each other somewhat similar to that existing between the four Gospels of the New Testament. In the gospels we have a quartet of evangelical biographers, all giving glimpses of the Lord's life, no two in just the same way. They did not even record any single event of that marvelous life of God incarnate in the same way; nor did they report verbatim any discourse of the divine Master. The evangelists Matthew, Mark, Luke, and John are like the four parts in some sublime musical composition. Each part differs from the other, yet together they form a most perfect harmony because they are arranged by one master musician. Each part is perfect in itself, yet requires the others to give the intended fullness. The one part expresses sweetness; the other, strength; another, pathos; and still another, profundity. Each part is essential to the proper expression of the other three and in the combination of the four we have the full, grand harmony. So the four Gospels, though differing, are all the compositions of one author—the Holy Spirit. Each is perfect, yet requires what the others contain to give to the fourfold record the surpassing beauty that every anointed eye beholds in the four evangelists. Each record, being perfectly proportioned to the others, produces that sublime anthem of praise to Heaven's beloved One of whom they speak.

And He was *the* King. In the two books into which we are about to glance we have kings—some comparatively good, and others exceedingly bad; some who made fair beginnings, and foul endings; others who commenced badly, but made a good finish. All, however, came short of God's glory and the divine ideal of what a king should be. He who was, according to the expectation of the Gentile magi, "born King of the Jews," and to the Jew Nathanael "the King of Israel," fulfilled that ideal perfectly. So He is called by Jehovah "My King." And in the fast-approaching day of His kingdom and power He will be known and acknowledged as King of nations (see Matthew 2:2; John 1:49; Psalm 2:6; Revelation 15:3).

Let us now look at the real differences between the Kings and Chronicles, and their significance.

Author's Introduction

In the LXX (Septuagint) 1 and 2 Kings are called "The third and fourth of the Kingdoms." Originally, in the Hebrew, they were one book like 1 and 2 Samuel. In the *Numerical Bible* Grant wrote, "Samuel and Kings, as we name them, should be, however, as they were originally, but one book each" (volume II, Page 287). The opening word of 1 Kings, Now, indicates that it is really a continuation of Samuel. The history recorded in 1 and 2 Kings is carried on past the middle of the captivity, and ends with Jehoiachin restored to liberty, and his throne set above that of the other kings that were in Babylon—a beautiful, though perhaps faint, shadow of Israel's restoration and exaltation in the coming millennial day. This, as someone has said, is "in happy consonance with its design." It is as "the first ray of God's returning favor," a slight pledge that David's seed and kingdom would (as God said), in spite of past failure, endure forever. Fausset said, in reference to Kings relation to Chronicles, "The language of Kings bears traces of an earlier date. Chaldee forms are rare in Kings, numerous in Chronicles, which has also Persicisms not found in Kings."

The writer of the books of the Kings is not known. The Talmud ascribes it to Jeremiah, which seems somewhat unlikely since the thirty-seventh year of Jehoiachin (the last date in the book) would be sixty-six years after his call to the prophetic office. Besides, the prophet probably died in Egypt with God's rebellious people, whom he so deeply loved and served. On the other hand, as Fausset stated, "The absence of mention of Jeremiah in Kings, though he was so prominent in the reigns of the last four kings, is just what we might expect if Jeremiah be the author of Kings." He remarks further: "In favor of Jeremiah's authorship is the fact that certain words are used only in Kings and in Jeremiah: *baqubuqu,* cruse (1 Kings 14:3; Jeremiah 19:1, 10); *yagab,* husbandman

(2 Kings 25:12; Jeremiah 52:16); *chabah,* hide (1 Kings 22:25; Jeremiah 49:10); *avar,* to bind (2 Kings 25:7; Jeremiah 39:7)."

But whoever the inspired penman may have been, he evidently wrote with a different purpose in view than the author of the Chronicles, who was probably Ezra, the priest. Two names, Akkub and Talmon, found in 1 Chronicles 9:17–18, and mentioned in Nehemiah 12:25–26 as being porters "in the days of Nehemiah, and of Ezra the priest," and Zer-ubbabel's name with that of others in 1 Chronicles 3:19, prove the writer lived and wrote after the restoration. The fact that the close of Chronicles and opening of Ezra overlap indicates one common author—as Luke and the Acts. Both 1 Chronicles 29:7 and Ezra 2:69 mention the Persian coin *daric* (dram). "The high priest's genealogy is given in the descending line, ending with the captivity, in 1 Chronicles 6:1–15. In Ezra 7:1–5, in the ascending line from Ezra himself to Aaron is given, abridged by the omission of many links, as the writer in Chronicles had already given a complete register" (Fausset). So if a prophet (Jeremiah) wrote the Kings, and a *priest* (Ezra) wrote the Chronicles, it would readily account for the ministry of the prophets being so prominent in the former book, and of the priests and Levites in the latter. It might also furnish the key as to the meaning of the marked differences in many portions of the two records.

1 and 2 Chronicles, like Samuel and Kings, were originally one book. They are called in the LXX *Paraleipomena,* or "Supplements". In Hebrew they are called "Words," or "Acts of Days." Its real history (after the genealogies) begins with the overthrow of Saul (1 Chronicles 10), and reads, almost word for word, like the concluding chapter of 1 Samuel, with this marked difference: Saul's body is mentioned in 1 Samuel 31:10 whereas in 1 Chronicles 10:10 his *head* alone is spoken of. In Chronicles there is also a comment on the cause of his

death, not found in Samuel, which would appear to indicate the author's desire to point out moral lessons in his "supplements" (1 Chronicles 10:13–14). These practical reflections are frequent in Chronicles; in Kings they rarely occur.

There are other marked differences between the two books, and all in perfect keeping with the design of each—divergent, though not contradictory—historian. Let us note a few of the most prominent. Second Samuel 24:24 says "David bought the threshingfloor [of Araunah] and the oxen for fifty shekels of silver"; 1 Chronicles 21:25 says, "David gave to Ornan for the place [not the threshing-floor and oxen merely] six hundred shekels of gold by weight." The molten sea made by Solomon, 1 Kings 7:26 says, "contained two thousand baths." Second Chronicles 4:5 says "it received and held three thousand baths" (its capacity). Frequently Chronicles has "God" where Kings has "LORD" (see 2 Samuel 5:19–25; 1 Chronicles 14:10–16; 2 Samuel 7:3–4; 1 Chronicles 17:2–3, etc.). "House of God" is found seven times in Chronicles; in Kings, not once. In 1 Chronicles 14:3 there is no mention of David's concubines, as in 2 Samuel 5:13. Nor does Chronicles mention his sin with Bathsheba, nor his son Amnon's crime against Tamar, nor Absalom's rebellion, nor Sheba's revolt. The idolatries of Solomon and some of the early kings of Judah are less detailed in Chronicles than in Kings; Chronicles, in fact, scarcely hints at Solomon's sin. Nor does it mention his somewhat questionable act of offering incense "upon the altar that was before the LORD" (1 Kings 9:25). Hezekiah's failure, too, is only briefly touched on in Chronicles. Yet we must not think that there was any attempt made on the part of the writer of Chronicles to pass over, or wink at, the sins of the house of David. He records Hanani's reproof of Asa, on which Kings is silent; also, Jehoram's murder of his brethren, and his idolatry. Nor does Kings mention Joash's apostasy and murder of Zechariah, Amaziah's sin of idolatry, nor Uzziah's sin of sacrilege. On the other hand, the refreshing account of Manasseh's repentance is peculiar to Chronicles; yet no mention is made in that book of the liberation of the captive Jehoiachin.

Kings gives only seven verses to Uzziah's reign, and but five to righteous Jotham's. Chronicles, on the other hand, summarizes Jehoiakim's reign in four verses, and Jehoiachin's in two. Israel is in the background in Chronicles; Judah and Jerusalem are (with the priests and Levites) its principal subject. However in Kings, Israel and her prophets (as Ahijah, Elijah, Elisha, Jonah, etc.), are prominent.

Another marked distinction between these two interesting books is the sources from which their writers obtained their material. In Kings it is evidently always derived from state records such as "the book of the acts of Solomon" (1 Kings 11:41); "the book of the chronicles of the kings of Judah" (1 Kings 14:29); "the book of the chronicles of the kings of Israel" (1 Kings 14:19), etc. Chronicles embodies more the writings of (or selections from) individuals such as "Samuel the seer," "Nathan the prophet," "Gad the seer," "the prophecy of Ahijah the Shilonite," "the visions of Iddo the seer," "the book of Shemaiah the prophet," "the story of the prophet Iddo," "the book of Jehu the son of Hanani," "Isaiah the prophet," etc. (1 Chronicles 29:29; 2 Chronicles 9:29; 12:15; 13:22; 20:34; 26:22).

The explanation of all this seems to be that the author of Kings wrote his book in Judah, where he would have access to the national archives; while the writer of Chronicles probably compiled his histories from the above-mentioned prophetical writings that were carried with the exiles to Babylon, or obtained after their restoration to the land. This would make the Chronicles peculiarly the book of the remnant;

Author's Introduction

while the Kings would be more for the nation at large, particularly Israel. And if this be so, it would explain why the sins of the earlier kings are veiled in Chronicles, and those of some of the later ones detailed. Being under Gentile domination, the Israelites were more or less in communication with them, and in all probability they would come in contact with these records of the Hebrew kings. Their later history would be better known to Gentiles, and it would be well for them to know just why they were permitted to destroy Jerusalem and hold the nation in bondage; hence the record of the sins of Josiah, Amaziah, Uzziah, and others. There was no need to record the sins of David, Solomon, and their immediate successors, as this did not in any way concern the Gentiles. It was probably in view of Gentile readers that *God* is so frequently used in Chronicles, instead of His covenant name *Jehovah,* that they might know that He is "not the God of the Jews only, but of the Gentiles also." This reaching out to the Gentiles is the branches of the blessing of Joseph beginning to hang over the wall (Genesis 49:22). Also perhaps this is the reason for the genealogical record given in 1 Chronicles 1 where we read of some people who are not of Israel, but all extending back to Adam, common father of us all. Note, too, in view of this, Asa's crushing defeat of Zerah the Ethiopian, recorded only in Chronicles, and his reproof by the prophet for relying on the king of Syria; Jehoshaphat's triumph over the vast allied forces of Moab and Ammon; *God's* (not *Jehovah's*) helping Uzziah against the Philistines, Arabians, and Mehunims, and the Ammonites giving him gifts; Jotham's victory over the Ammonites, and their tribute of silver, and wheat, and barley, rendered to him; and Manasseh's repentance (that the Gentiles might know God's grace) —all peculiar to Chronicles. On the other hand, Hezekiah's weakness in first yielding to, and afterward rebelling against,

Sennacherib (2 Kings 18) is carefully excluded from Chronicles. God never needlessly exposes the faults of His servants to the stranger. "Tell it not in Gath, publish it not in the streets of Askelon," is His beautiful principle of action in such cases.

Then as to Kings, the sins of the house of David in its earlier history are faithfully and minutely recorded, that both Judah and Israel (for whose reading the book was primarily intended) might know the reason for their debased and divided condition. The book gives mainly the history of the northern kingdom, and it is delightful to see that though the terrible sins of its rulers are exposed, any acts of grace or goodness on the part of them or the people are also carefully recorded (see 2 Kings 6:8–23, etc.). Prophets were prominent among the Israelites because they had cut themselves off from the ministry of the priests and Levites (which naturally connected itself with the temple at Jerusalem), and God made merciful provision for their spiritual needs by the prophetic ministry of such men as Elijah, etc.

These, I believe, are the real differences between the Kings and Chronicles. They are by no means so easily defined as those existing between the four Evangelists, and I do not profess to explain all of the many and marked variations that have been pointed out. The differences that have been offered in the foregoing may not be entirely satisfactory to all, but if they afford the reader any real help or clue to further discoveries in this direction, the author's main object will have been accomplished. What both writer and reader most need in these studies is to be more in touch with that blessed Master who, in the midst of His disciples, "opened their understanding, that they might understand the Scriptures."

Before closing this Introduction, it might be well to say a word about the authenticity of these books of Kings and

Author's Introduction

Chronicles. As to the first, our Lord stamped it with His divine authority by referring repeatedly to it, as in the cases of the widow of Sarepta and Naaman the Syrian. Paul referred to Elijah's intercession against Israel, and James mentioned his earnest prayer in connection with drought and rain. Hebrews 11:35 alludes to the raising of the Shunammite's son; and Jezebel is mentioned by our Lord in Revelation 2:20. Christ stamped the book of Chronicles with the seal of inspiration by alluding to the queen of Sheba's visit to King Solomon, and the martyrdom of Zechariah, "slain between the temple and the altar" (Matthew 23:35).

The histories as given in these books are likewise confirmed by both Egyptian and Assyrian monumental records; Rehoboam being mentioned on Syrian monuments, and Omri, Jehu, Menahem, Hoshea, and Hezekiah in the inscriptions on the monuments of the Assyrian Tiglath-pileser, Sargon, Sennacherib, and Esarhaddon. But Scripture, like its great subject, Christ, neither receives nor requires "testimony from men." The monuments do not prove Scripture to be true; it is only proved, when they agree with the Bible, that *they* are true, and not lies. As we read God's word, "we believe and are sure," because "holy men of God," who wrote these records, "spake as they were moved by the Holy Ghost" (2 Peter 1: 21). True, God's Word is called "prophecy" in that verse, but it has been aptly said that "*history* as written by the prophets is retroverted *prophecy.*" "Moses and the Prophets" (like "the Law and the Prophets") means the Pentateuch, the Old Testament historical books, and the writings generally designated as "the Prophets." And "the prophecy came not in old time by the will of man." So we unhesitatingly declare ourselves, like Paul of old, as "believing *all* things which are written in the law and in the prophets" (Acts 24:14).

CHRONOLOGICAL TABLE

The following is a listing, of the kings of Judah subsequent to the reigns of Saul, David, and Solomon, each of which lasted forty years (1051 B.C. to 931 B.C.).

B.C.	King	Length of reign in years
931	Rehoboam	17
913	Abijah	3
911	Asa	41
870	Jehoshaphat	25
848	Jehoram	8 — Evil
841	Ahaziah	1 — Evil
841	(Athaliah)	6
835	Jehoash	40 Good to bad
796	Amaziah	29 Start Good — End bad
792	Uzziah	52
750	Jotham	16
735	Ahaz	16 Bad
716	Hezekiah	29
697	Manasseh	55
643	Amon	2
641	Josiah	31 Last Great King Reformed
609	Jehoahaz	3 months Evil
609	Jehoiakim	11
598	Jehoiachin	3 months
597	Zedekiah	11
586	Jerusalem taken	

REHOBOAM

Liberator, or enlarger, of the people
(1 Kings 12: 1–24; 14: 21–31; 2 Chronicles 10–12)

CONTEMPORARY PROPHET: Shemaiah

In the multitude of people is the king's honor: but in the want of people is the destruction of the prince.

Proverbs 14: 28

Rehoboam was not what we call a strong character. He was, in the beginning of his reign at least, as his own son Abijah said to Jeroboam, "young [inexperienced] and tenderhearted, and could not withstand [the troublers of his kingdom]" (2 Chronicles 13:7). Why Solomon should have chosen him as his successor is not clear. It is difficult to believe that he had no other sons; yet it is a fact that Rehoboam is the only one mentioned (1 Chronicles 3:10). His father seems to have had misgivings concerning his ability to rule the kingdom (see Ecclesiastes 2:18–19; 4:13–16). And it was probably not a question of favoritism; for Pharaoh's daughter, and not Naamah the Ammonitess (Rehoboam's mother), appears to have been Solomon's preferred wife. But if Rehoboam was his only son, he had no choice; so we read "Rehoboam his son reigned in his stead" (1 Kings 11:43).

Weakness and vacillation marked his reign from the beginning. His going to Shechem to be crowned was evidently a concession to conciliate the already disaffected tribes to the north. He might have succeeded in his efforts to allay the dissatisfaction caused by the enforced levy of labor by his father (see 1 Kings 11:28), had he wisely and humbly heeded the advice of the aged men who had been his father's honored counselors. They, from long experience, knew the temper of the people well. In petitioning for the lightening of their burdens, they were only doing what any people not reduced to the condition of slavery, or serfdom, might have asked. Had the newly crowned king granted them their reasonable demands and been kind to them and spoken pleasantly to them, they would, as the old cabinet ministers said, have been his loyal subjects forever. But he forsook their wise counsels. He was influenced by a handful of callow novices and young court favorites, who, like himself, thought more of the rights of the king than of his responsibility to govern righteously. So he replied with as rash and insolent a speech as was ever uttered from the throne to a civilized nation. The outraged people answered in the same spirit as the king; and we have the sad, ominous cry, "What portion have we in David? neither have we inheritance in the son of Jesse: to your tents, O Israel: now see to thine own house, David" (1 Kings 12:16; see also 2 Samuel 20:1).

Rehoboam

Though truly thankful to God that we are privileged to live under a form of government that gives us fullest freedom, we have no quarrel with absolute monarchy. But while God enjoins subjection to the powers that be, tyranny over the souls and bodies of men is nowhere countenanced in His word and rulers who attempt it must suffer the results. There are many proofs of this in Scripture, as in history. Government is of God and therefore of divine appointment; but God frowns on all abuse of power.

Rehoboam found it hard to believe that the ten tribes had really refused his yoke. He flattered himself, no doubt, that they would not dare to rebel against his authority. It could not be possible, he might have thought, that these provincials should not readily and meekly submit to his chastening with scorpions. So he confidently sent to them Hadoram to collect the imposed assessment. This ill-advised act brings matters to a crisis, and the old collector general, who had served in this office under Rehoboam's father Solomon and his grandfather David, is stoned by the exasperated people. So the king, who had boasted so haughtily that his "little finger" should be "thicker than his father's loins," ingloriously "made speed to get him up to his chariot, to flee to Jerusalem" (1 Kings 12:18).

It must have been evident to him now that the rebellion was a very real and formidable one, and not a mere passing wave of discontent that would quickly die away of itself and be forgotten. But such an immense loss, such terrible results occurring so unexpectedly, were not so easily submitted to. Force may yet avail. There is the army, one hundred and eighty thousand strong. These malcontents would soon be made to feel the effect of its invincible power. Might must make right, if right cannot be demonstrated in any other way. But the God of peace, who loves His people even when

KINGS OF JUDAH

misguided and in error, warned the king of Judah (note the intentional limit of his title, 2 Chronicles 11:3) by the word of the man of God, Shemaiah, saying, "Ye shall not go up, nor fight against your brethren the children of Israel: return every man to his house; for this thing is from me" (1 Kings 12:24).

Under the government of God this division of the kingdom was the punishment for the sins of Solomon (1 Kings 11:29–33), occasioned by the folly of Rehoboam; it must therefore stand. To fight to bring back the unity of the nation, good as the purpose might seem, was to fight against God. Rehoboam ought to have been thankful that God's love to David had left him even two tribes. And he appears to have been, for the two tribes "hearkened therefore to the word of the LORD," He proceeded to secure what had been left him. He built, or garrisoned, fifteen cities within his decreased territory, "and he fortified the strong holds, and put captains in them, and store of victuals, and of oil and wine. And in every several city he put shields and spears, and made them exceeding strong" (2 Chronicles 11:11–12). The successful rebel may sometimes turn *invader,* and Rehoboam (wiser now) guarded against this. There was war between him and the insurrectionist leader Jeroboam all their days, and the son of Solomon had to vigilantly guard what remained to him.

The priests and Levites remained faithful to Jehovah, to His house and worship at Jerusalem, and to the house of David, which was by the election of God the royal one. They left the land of Israel to dwell in Judah and Jerusalem. Others too, who had set their hearts to seek the God of Israel, deserted the cause of the secessionists, and flocked to Rehoboam's standard. For three years all went well, and they walked "in the way of David and Solomon." But their goodness (like all that is of the creature merely) was as the early dew and like the morning cloud, and passed quickly away. Subdued, no doubt, and humbled by the loss of the greater portion of his kingdom, Rehoboam walked for a time in fear and dependence. But even serious lessons like this are soon forgotten by most, and before five years had passed both king and people had lapsed so far into idolatry as to be brought to the very verge of apostasy from Jehovah.

> And Judah did evil in the sight of the LORD, and they provoked him to jealousy with their sins which they had committed, above all that their fathers had done. For they also built them high places, and images, and groves, on every high hill, and under every green tree. And there were also sodomites [men consecrated to impurity] in the land: and they did according to all the abominations of the nations which the LORD cast out before the children of Israel (1 Kings 14:22–24).

And for this reason God sent Shishak king of Egypt against them. Solomon had joined affinity with Pharaoh by marrying his daughter. Whether Solomon did this merely to please himself, or with the expectation of strengthening his kingdom by an alliance with so powerful a country, it all came to nothing, as do all such ways where God's word is disobeyed or ignored.

Shishak overthrew Pharaoh, the father-in-law of Solomon, thus ending that dynasty. He became the new king who did not know Solomon nor his successor. Influenced probably by Jeroboam, he marched against Jerusalem with a vast army of twelve hundred chariots and sixty thousand horsemen, besides an innumerable host of footmen (2 Chronicles 12:3). Realizing the utter hopelessness of his position, and not having faith in God, Rehoboam offered no resistance to the advance of Shishak. In fear for his life, he huddled with the princes of Judah at Jerusalem and awaited the coming of the Egyptian army.

It is now God's time to speak to their consciences, and Shemaiah the prophet appeared before them with this message of conviction: "Thus saith the LORD, Ye have forsaken me, and therefore have I also left you in the hand of Shishak." (12:5). They humbled themselves then and said, "The LORD is righteous," and a partial deliverance was promised them. God said, "I will not destroy them." "The princes of Israel and the king humbled themselves," says the Word. It would seem the princes took the lead (from their being mentioned first) in this humiliating, yet becoming, confession. The king was slower, the roots of his former arrogance still lingering unjudged within his heart.

Note what God says: "I will not destroy them" (12:7). Shishak was only His whip, like the Assyrian at a later date, whom God, by His prophet Isaiah, called "the rod of mine anger" and "a razor that is hired." In calamities like these, it is necessary to see beyond the instrument, and know the hand that uses it for blessing. But though their lives were spared, they must become servants (tributary) to Shishak, "That they may know," God says, "my service, and the service of the kingdoms of the countries." When one is truly submissive, he will find the Lord's yoke is easy; if His saint refuses to wear it, he must learn by humiliating and painful experience what the yoke of the enemy is like. So Shishak took away all the temple treasures, and those of the royal palace. He also took with him the five hundred shields of gold that Solomon had made. Rehoboam made in their stead shields of bronze, and with these he pathetically tried to keep up former appearances. It is like souls who, when despoiled of their freshness and power by the enemy, laboriously endeavor to keep up an outward appearance of spiritual prosperity. Or like a fallen

Rehoboam

church, stripped of its strength and robbed of its purity, it seeks to hide its helplessness and cover its nakedness with the tinsel of ritualism and spurious revivalism. It looks for anything that promises to give it some appearance of justification for saying, "I am rich, and increased with goods."

There is little more to say of Rehoboam. Whatever was in his father's mind when naming him "Liberator" or "Enlarger of the People," he failed utterly to become either. He enslaved the nation to Shishak by his sins, and decreased the numerical strength of his kingdom by more than three million through his folly at the very outset of his reign. He followed his father's shameful example in taking many wives. He displayed wisdom however in distributing his sons over the countries of Judah and Benjamin, placing them in the garrison towns, and providing them food in abundance (2 Chronicles 11:23). He probably remembered and was desirous to avoid such scenes as had occurred at the close of his grandfather David's life in connection with his sons (see 1 Kings 2). Would God that Christians had always as much *spiritual* wisdom as Rehoboam manifested *natural* wisdom in this. Were God's people well fed with truth, and consecrated to Christ through the various services of His kingdom, there would be less strife among us. But sadly, it is still too often true that "the children of this world are in their generation wiser than the children of light" (Luke 16:8). Rehoboam's wisdom was rewarded when, at the end of his seventeen years' reign, his son Abijah quietly assumed the crown without opposition from his many brothers.

Rehoboam died at the age of fifty-eight. The Spirit's last comment on his character is significant: "And he did evil because he prepared not his heart to seek the LORD" (2 Chronicles 12:14). There we are told in a single sentence the whole secret of his failure, both as king of Judah, and servant of

Jehovah, who gave him this exalted position—"He [applied] not his heart to seek [Jehovah]." May God in His grace, help us to apply our hearts to seek first and always His kingdom and righteousness. Only so shall we be kept from evil, and preserved from making the record of our lives read anything like Rehoboam's—one sad succession of decline and failure.

ABIJAH

Jehovah is my Father
(1 Kings 15:1–8; 2 Chronicles 13)

CONTEMPORARY PROPHET: Iddo

Great deliverance giveth he to his king; and showeth mercy to his anointed, to David, and to his seed for evermore.

Psalm 18:50

Abijah's reign was a brief one. He outlived his father Rehoboam by only three short years. His mother Maachah was a daughter or granddaughter of Absalom. (We should remember that family relations are not so scrupulously mentioned in Scripture as it is our custom now to do. Thus blood relations are often mentioned as "brother" and ancestors as "father" or "mother.") Abijah (Abijam in Kings) was thus de-

KINGS OF JUDAH

scended from David on both his father's and his mother's side. His mother however turned out to be an idolatress (1 Kings 15:13). The form of her name *Maachah,* which means "oppressor," is altered in Chronicles to *Michaiah*—"Who is like God?" She is said here, too, to be a daughter of *Uriel,* meaning "light" or "fire of God." The reason for this will be understood by referring to the Author's Introduction. There is also no account of Abijah's wickedness in Chronicles. In Kings, on the other hand, there is nothing recorded of him but his sin. "He walked," it says there, "in all the sins of his father, which he had done before him: and his heart was not perfect with the LORD his God, as the heart of David his father" (1 Kings 15:3).

He was evidently a man of considerable spirit, for he had barely settled himself in his throne before he began a war with his father's old adversary Jeroboam. His army numbered 400,000 "chosen men," while Jeroboam's was 800,000 "mighty men of valour" (2 Chronicles 13:2–3).

A wonderful battle ensued, and it was preceded by a very wonderful speech from Abijah. He stood on the top of Mount Zemaraim, in Mount Ephraim, somewhere along the northern border of his kingdom. For terseness, accusation, warning, and appeal the address is unsurpassed by anything in any literature of any time (2 Chronicles 13:4–12). Its merit was recognized even in his own day, for the prophet Iddo did not neglect to record the eloquent king's sayings. We shall not attempt to analyze it. Nor does it require any analysis for it is simple as it is weighty and powerful. Though true in all its statements, it lacks frankness. He said,

> Hear me, thou Jeroboam, and all Israel; Ought ye not to know that the LORD God of Israel gave the kingdom over Israel to David for ever, even to him and to his sons by a covenant of salt? Yet Jeroboam the son of Nebat, the servant of Solomon

Abijah

the son of David, is risen up, and hath rebelled against his lord (4–6).

The gathered hosts who listened to him knew well the truth of this. But, either intentionally or unconsciously, he ignored the root of all this strife—his grandfather's sins. He also ignored the fact that God had forbidden his father Rehoboam to make war on the separated tribes, saying, "This thing [the schism] is from me." He knew how to make his own position appear right and good, but he completely ignored the judgment of God on his own tribes and on the house of David because of its own sins; how unlike the humble and confessing spirit of his father David. His speech reflected wisdom, but a cold wisdom apart from the spirit of grace.

But he continued: "And there are gathered unto him vain men, the children of Belial, and have strengthened themselves against Rehoboam the son of Solomon." Strong words these, spoken before an army of valiant men twice the size of his own! He was determined to make them realize that however strong they are, their origin in separation from his own tribes is not of God. This, of course, would also greatly strengthen his own adherents, and he was doubtless speaking for their ears as well as for those of his enemies. Ignoring the judgment of God on the nation, he made the plea that his father Rehoboam "was young and tenderhearted, and could not withstand them. And now ye think to withstand the kingdom of the LORD in the hand of the sons of David." He seemed to say, You might deter my fainthearted father from punishing you and reducing you to submission, but you have a different man to deal with now.

Then follows that which, together with Jehovah's love for the house of David, secured Abijah's victory and Jeroboam's awful defeat:

And ye be a great multitude, and there are with you golden calves, which Jeroboam made you for gods. Have ye not cast out the priests of the LORD, the sons of Aaron, and the Levites, and have made you priests after the manner of the nations of other lands? so that whosoever cometh to consecrate himself with a young bullock and seven rams, the same may be a priest of them that are no gods. But as for us, [Jehovah] is our God, and we have not forsaken him. [However true this might be *outwardly,* we have seen already the Spirit's testimony as to the *inward* or real condition in Judah as declared in 1 Kings 14:22–25.] And the priests, which minister unto the LORD, are the sons of Aaron, and the Levites wait upon their business: And they burn unto [Jehovah] every morning and every evening burnt sacrifices and sweet incense: the shewbread also they set in order upon the pure table; and the candlestick of gold with the lamps thereof to burn every evening: for we keep the charge of [Jehovah] our God; but ye have forsaken him. And, behold, God himself is with us for our captain, and his priests, with sounding trumpets to cry a alarm against you. [Then he closed with a brief but eloquent appeal:] Children of Israel, fight ye not against [Jehovah] the God of your fathers; for ye shall not prosper! (2 Chronicles 13:8–12)

On the one hand, all this is inspiring; on the other, had it been true in their heart-relations with Jehovah as it was true in the outward sense, they would not have been found facing their brethren for battle and about to be engaged in dreadful carnage. But while God could not have put His seal on the state of Abijah's soul and the tribes with him, He must vindicate the righteousness of all that is said against Jeroboam and his followers. So though "orthodoxy" be away from God in heart, yet its battle against antichrists must for the time being be acknowledged and helped. The house of David is loved,

Abijah

and must be sustained—Christ is dear to God, and all who fight for Him must be upheld, though God may have something against them too. So Abijah won a great victory, and Israel suffered a most humiliating defeat. More than half their army is slain, and it was more than sixteen years before they again attempted to make war on the house of David. "Thus the children of Israel were brought under at that time, and the children of Judah prevailed, because they relied upon the LORD the God of their fathers" (18). God acknowledges whatever good He can find among His people.

Abijah also took three cities, Bethel, Jeshanah, and Ephron with their dependent villages from Israel. Neither did Jeroboam ever recover from the effects of his defeat and soon after he was struck by Jehovah and died.

When not more than forty years old, Abijah died. Like his father before him, he was unfortunate in not having a good mother. He is called Abijam in Kings. God would not let His name be called upon him there, because there it is only the dark side of his life which is told. God is jealous of His name. It is a holy name, and He would not have it dishonored by the sins of those who are called by that name. May all His people everywhere give heed to this. The holy name of Christ (*Christian*) is given us. May we never by any act of ours bring a stain of reproach on it!

ASA

Healing or Cure
(1 Kings 15:9–24; 2 Chronicles 14–16)

CONTEMPORARY PROPHETS: Azariah son of Oded, Hanani, Jehoram

Better is a poor and a wise child, than an old and foolish king, who will no more be admonished.

Ecclesiastes 4:13

*A*sa's name means "healing" or "cure," and indicates the reformation and consequent rest effected by him during the earlier portion of his reign. He made a most excellent beginning.

And Asa did that which was good and right in the eyes of the LORD his God: For he took away the altars of the strange gods, and the high places, and brake down the images, and cut down the groves: And commanded Judah to seek the LORD God of their fathers, and to do the law and the commandment. Also he took away out of all the cities of Judah the high places and the images: and the kingdom was quiet before him (2 Chronicles 14:2–5).

But he did not stop there; he did more:

He built fenced cities in Judah: for the land had rest, and he had no war in those years; because the LORD had given him rest. Therefore he said unto Judah, Let us build these cities, and make about them walls, and towers, gates, and bars, while the land is yet before us; because we have sought the LORD our God, we have sought him, and he hath given us rest on every side (6–7).

He was no mere iconoclast. If he had the zeal to break down the images, he had also the wisdom to build fortified cities. To expose evil is very well, but to furnish the soul with truth is what protects it from the invasion of the enemy. They redeemed the time, as we are bidden to do in Ephesians 5:16, "Redeeming the time, because the days are evil." So God was with them. Encouraged by the king's words and example, the people entered heartily into the blessed work of building and fortifying.

Well would it have been for the sixteenth century churches had they been as wise after the Reformation, during the rest that followed, and built and fortified themselves in defense of "the faith once for all delivered to the saints." But alas, they slept; and when the hosts of worldliness, ritualism, and rationalism appeared at their borders, they were utterly unprepared and powerless to repel them. They were not, like Judah, prepared and able to resist the enemy when he came.

> And there came out against them Zerah the Ethiopian with an host of a thousand thousand, and three hundred chariots; and came unto Mareshah. Then Asa went out against him, and they set the battle in array in the valley of Zephathah at Mareshah. And Asa cried unto the LORD his God, and said, LORD, it is nothing with thee to help, whether with many, or with them that have no power: help us, O LORD our God; for we rest on thee, and in thy name we go against this multitude. O LORD, thou art our God; let not man [Enosh, frail, mortal man] prevail against thee. So the LORD smote the Ethiopians before Asa, and before Judah; and the Ethiopians fled (9–12).

The monuments do not make clear just who this Zerah was. A king called *Azerch Amar* was reigning over Ethiopia about this time, and the inspired chronicler may have given the Hebrew form of his name.

The greatness of Egypt, which Shishak had raised, diminished at his death. His immediate successors were of no note in the monuments. Zerah seems to have taken advantage of Egypt's weakness to extort permission to march his enormous force, composed of the same nationalities (Ethiopians and Lubians) as those of the preceding invader, Shishak, through Egypt into Judah (Fausset).

Others identify him with Osorkon II, one of Shishak's successors. He was son-in-law to Osorkon I, king of Egypt, and ruled in right of his wife. He was, if this be true, an Ethiopian ruling his own country jointly with that of his wife's (Egypt). And the invasion would then probably be caused by Asa's refusal to continue paying the tribute imposed on his grandfather Rehoboam by Shishak. But it was one thing for Shishak to invade the land of Judah "because they had transgressed against the LORD" (2 Chronicles 12:2), and quite a different matter when Zerah came against them unprovoked. He met his just punishment from God, who loves and defends His people; he was defeated therefore, and his immense army, numbering more than a million, was utterly destroyed.

Asa's faith rose to blessed heights on this occasion. Though he was in control of a fine army of over a half million "mighty men of valour," he took the place of entire dependence on God, and made the conflict a matter between God and the enemy. Such faith can never be disappointed.

On Asa's triumphant return to Jerusalem the Spirit of God came on *Azariah* ("whom Jehovah helps") the son of Oded, and he went to meet him, not as a court flatterer, but with a solemn yet cheering word of admonition (2 Chronicles 15). He said, "Hear ye me, Asa, and all Judah and Benjamin; The LORD is with you, while ye be with him; and if ye seek him, he will be found of you; but if ye forsake him, he will forsake you." It was "a word in season"; for it has been truly said that we are never in greater danger than immediately after some great success, even though it be truly from God in answer to genuine faith. David is a sad example. In the chapters preceding that which records his sin with Bathsheba (2 Samuel 11) we read of his continued series of brilliant victories over his enemies. He defeated and subdued the Philistines, Moab, Hadarezer king of Zobah, the Syrians, the Ammonites, and Amalek. Then, as if resting in these victories, his watchfulness was relaxed and the mighty fell. And Asa, his descendant of the fifth generation, was graciously warned of God lest he should also fall into similar condemnation.

Azariah then reminded them that in days gone by ("hath

been," 2 Chronicles 15:3, should be "was"—evidently referring to the days of the Judges) when in apostasy and distress, the people turned to Jehovah God of Israel (see Judges 5). They sought Him and He was found of them. "Be ye strong therefore," he said, "and let not your hands be weak: for your work shall be rewarded." Asa had probably met with opposition in his reformatory work, and was in danger of failing to continue it to its completion. So he was exhorted to be firm, for there would be a sure reward for his deeds of restoration of the uncorrupted worship of Jehovah in his realm.

> And when Asa heard these words, and the prophecy of Oded the prophet [the Vulgate and Syriac manuscripts read, "Azariah son of Oded"], he took courage, and put away the abominable idols out of all the land of Judah and Benjamin, and out of the cities which he had taken from mount Ephraim, and renewed the altar of the LORD, that was before the porch of the LORD (2 Chronicles 15:8).

This was the altar on which Solomon offered burnt offerings when he brought his Egyptian bride into the house that he had built for her (2 Chronicles 8:12). It had evidently been removed, or allowed to fall into disuse or decay before being rebuilt by Asa.

His great victory over Zerah had its effect on many among the revolted tribes (for nothing wins God's people like God's blessing), and "they fell to him out of Israel in abundance, when they saw that the LORD his God was with him" (15:9). Stimulated by these additions to their ranks, the people entered into a covenant "to seek the LORD God of their fathers with all their heart and with all their soul." The tide of reformation ran high—too high, it is to be feared; for they determined "that whosoever would not seek the LORD

God of Israel should be put to death, whether small or great, whether man or woman." This severity was hardly appropriate coming from a people who had only a short time before been themselves guilty of just such omission. They were excessively demonstrative also. "And they sware unto the LORD with a loud voice, and with shouting, and with trumpets, and with cornets." Such demonstrations were no new thing in Israel. They had been heard before at Sinai and elsewhere, and always with like results—more saying than doing; much promise, and little performance; great anticipation, and scant realization. But there was evident sincerity, and even reality, though mixed with much that was superficial. God, who can discern what is of Himself even when mingled with what is only of the flesh, rewarded them. "And all Judah rejoiced at the oath: for they had sworn with all their heart, and sought him with their whole desire; and he was found of them: and the LORD gave them rest round about" (15).

Asa was no respecter of persons. He spared not his own mother (or grandmother), but deposed her for her idolatry. "And also concerning Maachah the mother of Asa the king, he removed her from being queen, because she had made an idol in a grove: and Asa cut down her idol, and stamped it, and burnt it at the brook Kidron." It is in a man's own family circle that his faithfulness is put fairly to the test. Levi was "proved at Massah," where he "said unto his father and to his mother, I have not seen him; neither did he acknowledge his brethren, nor knew his own children" (Deuteronomy 33:8–9). Gideon too began his work for God by breaking down the altar of Baal that his father had set up. And in the apostolic church men could not serve as elders or deacons if they had not properly regulated homes. And He who was called "Faithful and True" said, when occasion required, "Who is my mother? and who are my brethren?" (Matthew 12:48.)

Asa

"In the six and thirtieth year of the reign of Asa, Baasha king of Israel came up against Judah, and built Ramah, to the intent that he might let none go out or come in to Asa king of Judah" (2 Chronicles 16:1). This verse, when compared with 1 Kings 15:33 and 16:8, presents a chronological difficulty. Baasha must have been dead ten years before the thirty-sixth year of Asa's reign, according to the above references. And we cannot be always falling back, in these seeming discrepancies, on a supposed error in transcription. The only apparent way out of the difficulty is to take "the six and thirtieth year" to date from the beginning of Judah as a separate kingdom from Israel. This would make the event to occur in the sixteenth year of the actual reign of Asa and shortly after the occurrences of the preceding chapter. Ramah was on the high road from the northern kingdom. It would be natural for Baasha to take immediate steps to fortify this key city on the frontier, and thus check any further secessions to Asa from his dominion.

> Then Asa brought out silver and gold out of the treasures of the house of the LORD and of the king's house, and sent to Benhadad king of Syria, that dwelt at Damascus, saying, There is a league between me and thee, as there was between my father and thy father: behold, I have sent thee silver and gold; go, break thy league with Baasha king of Israel, that he may depart from me (2 Chronicles 16:2–3).

It is difficult to account for this sudden defect in Asa's faith. He had only recently, with God's help, completely destroyed the immense army of Zerah the Ethiopian. Now, before an enemy not half so formidable, his faith fails, and he depends for deliverance on an arm of flesh. Had not his father Abijah, in dependence on the Lord, defeated a former army of Israel double the size of his own? It was the beginning of Asa's downfall; for though the desired deliverance was obtained (for "Benhadad hearkened unto King Asa," and Baasha "left off building of Ramah, and let his work cease"), it cost him the rebuke of God and wars to the end of his reign.

> And at that time Hanani the seer came to Asa king of Judah, and said unto him, Because thou hast relied on the king of Syria, and not relied on the LORD thy God, therefore is the host of the king of Syria escaped out of thy hand. Were not the Ethiopians and the Lubim a huge host, with very many chariots and horsemen? yet, because thou didst rely on the LORD, he delivered them into thine hand. For the eyes of the LORD run to and fro throughout the whole earth, to shew himself strong in the behalf of them whose heart is perfect [or sincere] toward him. Herein thou hast done foolishly: therefore from henceforth thou shalt have wars (16:7–9).

"Therefore is the host of the king of Syria escaped out of thy hand." Instead of calling on Benhadad for help, Asa could have subdued him, as "escaped out of thy hand" implies. David had reigned over Damascus, and only in the days of Solomon's degeneracy did Syria begin to exist as a separate and independent kingdom (see 1 Kings 11:23–25). Its first king "was an adversary to Israel all the days of Solomon... and he abhorred Israel, and reigned over Syria." This continued to be the attitude of Syria toward Israel; but it was in God's heart to use Asa to destroy this heathen power, which in future days caused His people so much sorrow and distress (see 2 Kings 8:11–13). But he missed his opportunity; and when charged by Hanani with folly, he committed the seer to prison for his faithfulness. "Then Asa was wroth with the seer, and put him in a prison house; for he was in a rage with him because of this thing. And Asa oppressed some of the people the same time"—the seer's sympathizers, probably (2 Chronicles 16:10). His petty anger (at what he knew only too well to be the truth) betrayed a low condition of soul from which he never evidently recovered; and his end was humiliating as his beginning had been brilliant. "And Asa, in the thirty and ninth year of his reign, was diseased in his feet, until his disease was exceeding great: yet in his disease he sought not to the LORD, but to the physicians" (12). In all this record, let us hear and take to ourselves the Lord's word, "He that hath an ear to hear, let him hear."

It is easily seen why the chronicler should write of Asa's acts "first and last" (2 Chronicles 16:11). "Ye did run well: who did hinder you?" might be asked of many besides the Galatians and Asa. Important as a good beginning is, it is not all: we are called to run with endurance the race that is set before us. But when God's people become diseased in their feet, they cease to run well; and though they may try various expedients, such as ritualism, revivalism, the union of churches, etc., to recover themselves, they are every one of them physicians of no value. "Restore unto me the joy of thy salvation," wrote a notable backslider (Psalm 51:12). It is Jehovah who says through His prophet, "I will heal their backslidings."

There was a great funeral made over Asa, and he appears to have been sincerely lamented by his people.

> And Asa slept with his fathers, and died in the one and fortieth year of his reign. And they buried him in his own sepulchres, which he had made for himself in the city of David, and laid him in the bed which was filled with sweet odors and divers kinds of spices prepared by the apothecaries' art: and they made a very great burning for him (2 Chronicles 16:13–14).

Asa's history reveals his weaknesses: God, in His comments on his character, gives no hint of them (2 Chronicles 20:32; 21:12). He loves to commend whatever is lovely in His servants' lives, and only when necessary exposes their failures and follies. May we in this, as in all things else, be "imitators of God" (Ephesians 5:1).

Jeremiah 41:9 refers to a pit (or cistern) made by Asa "for fear of Baasha king of Israel." God would thus, in this incidental way, remind us by this last historical notice of king Asa what was the beginning of his decline—"the fear of man [which] bringeth a snare" (Proverbs 29:25).

JEHOSHAPHAT

He whom Jehovah judges
(1 Kings 15:24; 22:41–50; 2 Kings 8:16; 2 Chronicles 17:1–21:3)

CONTEMPORARY PROPHETS: Jehu son of Hanani, Jahaziel the Levite, Eliezer son of Dodavah

Mercy and truth preserve the king: and his throne is upholden by mercy.

Proverbs 20:28

he first thing recorded of Jehoshaphat is that he "strengthened himself against Israel. And he placed forces in all the fenced cities of Judah, and set garrisons in the land of Judah, and in the cities of Ephraim, which Asa his father had taken" (2 Chronicles 17:1–2). He began his reign with a determined opposition to the idolatrous northern kingdom.

KINGS OF JUDAH

This was in the fourth year of Ahab. A few years later all this opposition ceased, and we read, "Jehoshaphat made peace with the king of Israel" (1 Kings 22:44). This peace was brought about, evidently, by the marriage of Jehoshaphat's son Jehoram to Athaliah, daughter of Ahab and the notorious Jezebel. Alas for Jehoshaphat and his posterity, that he ever gave his consent to this unholy alliance, and made peace with him "who did evil in the sight of the LORD above all that were before him" (1 Kings 16:30)! But such is man, even at his best, "wherein is he to be accounted of?"

But like Asa his father, he made a bright beginning:

> And the LORD was with Jehoshaphat, because he walked in the first ways of his father David [that is, before his sin in the matter of Uriah the Hittite] and sought not unto Baalim; But sought to the LORD God of his father, and walked in his commandments, and not after the doings of Israel. Therefore the LORD stablished the kingdom in his hand; and all Judah brought to Jehoshaphat presents; and he had riches and honour in abundance. And his heart was lifted up [encouraged] in the ways of the LORD: moreover he took away the high places and groves out of Judah (2 Chronicles 17:3–6).

This last statement does not contradict what is said in 1 Kings 22:43. The high places and groves used for the worship of Baalim were removed; "nevertheless the high places [dedicated to Jehovah] were not taken away; for the people offered and burned incense [to the true God] yet in the high places" (compare 2 Chronicles 20:33). He abolished idolatry, but the people could not be brought to see the unlawfulness and danger of offering sacrifices elsewhere than at Jerusalem. Deuteronomy 12 condemned this practice, and it was probably to instruct the people regarding worship and related matters that he inaugurated the model itinerary described in 2 Chronicles 17:7–9.

> Also in the third year of his reign he sent to his princes, even to Benhail, and to Obadiah, and to Zechariah, and to Nethaneel, and to Michaiah to teach in the cities of Judah. And with them he sent Levites…and with them Elishama and Jehoram, priests. And they taught in Judah, and had the book of the law of the LORD with them, and went about throughout all the cities of Judah, and taught the people.

By this little group of princes, Levites, and priests—sixteen in all—Jehoshaphat did more toward impressing the surrounding nations with a sense of his power than the largest and best-equipped standing army could have secured to him.

And the fear of [Jehovah] fell upon all the kingdoms of the lands that were round about Judah, so that they made no war against Jehoshaphat. Also some of the Philistines brought Jehoshaphat presents and tribute silver; and the Arabians brought him flocks, seven thousand and seven hundred rams, and seven thousand and seven hundred he goats.

This was the promise of God, through Moses, fulfilled to the Israelites. If they diligently obeyed and stuck with Jehovah, He would, He said, "lay the fear of you and the dread of you upon all the land" (Deuteronomy 11:22–25). When the patriarch Jacob ordered his family to put away the strange gods that were among them, "the terror of God was upon the cities that were round about them" (Genesis 35:5). And it was when the infant church at Jerusalem "continued steadfastly in the apostles' doctrine and fellowship, and in breaking of bread, and in prayers," that "fear came upon every soul"

(Acts 2:42–43). In obedience is power, and only right makes might in the nation or church that has God for its help.

"And Jehoshaphat waxed great exceedingly; and he built in Judah castles, and cities of store. And he had much business in the cities of Judah." It was an era of great commercial prosperity, and the kingdom was in the zenith of its power and glory. He had an organized army of over a million men "ready prepared for the war" (2 Chronicles 17:12–19).

Then the cloud descended over this noonday splendor of the king and kingdom.

> Now Jehoshaphat had riches and honour in abundance, and [he allied himself with Ahab by marriage.] And after certain years he went down [yes, it was "down" morally, as well as topographically] to Ahab to Samaria. And Ahab killed sheep and oxen for him in abundance, and for the people that he had with him, and persuaded him to go up [against] with him to Ramoth-gilead. And Ahab king of Israel said to Jehoshaphat king of Judah, Wilt thou go with me to Ramoth-Gilead? And he answered him, I am as thou art, and my people as thy people; and we will be with thee in the war (2 Chronicles 18:1–3).

It was a sad come-down for the godly king of Judah. Think of him saying to a wicked idolater like Ahab, "I am as thou." And he not only put himself down to Ahab's base level, he compromised his people also by saying they were as Ahab's people all of whom, excepting seven thousand men, were bowing the knee to Baal. Such conduct and language from a man like Jehoshaphat seems almost incredible. But "who can understand his [own] errors?" It is often much more difficult to see our own mistakes, than those of others.

Ahab evidently had fears for Jehoshaphat's scruples of conscience, and was prepared to meet them. So the feast prepared for him and his group was given a religious character (the word for *killed* is *sacrificed*). An apostate people or church will go to almost any length of seeming compromise to entice and draw the faithful into fellowship or alliance with them. What must have godly men like Elijah thought of all this? It is little wonder that when fleeing from the murderous wrath of Jezebel he feared to trust himself anywhere within the realm of Judah (see 1 Kings 19:3–4. Beersheba was on Judah's southern border.) Many would, no doubt, loudly praise the king of Judah for what they would term his large-heartedness and freedom from bigotry. The four hundred false prophets (Israel's clergy) could also quote from Psalm 133, "Behold, how good and how pleasant it is for brethren to dwell together in unity!" and say how the world was growing better, and the millennium soon to come. Yes, and the cry today is for "union" (*unity* they know little of, and care less for), amalgamation, good fellowship. The false teachers cry, "away with dogma" (Scripture, they really mean), "let doctrine die the death, and let twentieth century enlightenment make us ashamed of the conduct of our forefathers who fought, suffered, and died for the truth." "What is truth?" was Pilate's idle question—the answer to which he had neither heart nor conscience—while before him Jesus witnessed that good confession, declaring what men of today would condemn as bigotry of the most pronounced kind: "To this end was I born, and for this cause came I into the world, that I should bear witness unto the truth. Every one that is of the truth heareth my voice" (John 18:37). But it is come to pass today that "truth is perished in the streets."

But to return to Jehoshaphat. He is not altogether at ease in his mind about this contemplated attack on Ramoth-gilead ("A fortress commanding Argob and the Jair towns, seized by Ben-hadad I from Omri." Josephus). His consent to accompany Ahab was, no doubt, hastily given, and probably during the warmth and excitement of the good fellowship at the banquet tendered in his honor. It is impossible not to violate a godly conscience, once we accept the fellowship of the wicked.

Too late Jehoshaphat inquired of Jehovah. A prophet, Micaiah, fearlessly foretold the failure of the enterprise. But he was only one against four hundred; "So the king of Israel and Jehoshaphat the king of Judah went up to Ramoth-gilead" (2 Chronicles 18:28). But for God's mercy Jehoshaphat would have lost his life. Jehovah heard his cry for help, and delivered him; "and Jehoshaphat the king of Judah returned to his house in peace to Jerusalem," a humbler, a wiser, and, we trust, a grateful man (19:1).

But God had a message of rebuke for him.

> And Jehu the son of Hanani the seer went out to meet him, and said to king Jehoshaphat, Shouldest thou help the ungodly, and love them that hate the LORD? therefore is wrath upon thee from before the LORD. Nevertheless there are good things found in thee, in that thou hast taken away the groves out of the land, and hast prepared thine heart to seek God (2 Chronicles 19:2–3).

Hanani, Jehu's father, had gone to prison for his faithfulness to Asa on a similar occasion, not fearing the wrath of the king (2 Chronicles 16:7–10). The son of Asa, unlike his father, did not persecute his reprover; but much humiliated by his late experience, it would seem from what immediately follows that he profited by the rebuke. "And Jehoshaphat dwelt at Jerusalem: and he went out again through the people from Beer-sheba to mount Ephraim, and brought them back unto the LORD God of their fathers." He "went out again." This implies that he had lapsed spiritually, and was now restored, repentant, and doing the "first works." The work of reforming the nation is resumed on his recovery. Like his great progenitor David, when the joy of God's salvation was restored to him, he vowed to "teach transgressors [God's] ways; and sinners shall be converted unto [Him]" (Psalm 51:12).

Jehoshaphat also set judges in all the fortified cities of the land. He charged them solemnly, saying, "Take heed what ye do: for ye judge not for man, but for the LORD, who is with you in the judgment. Wherefore now let the fear of the LORD be upon you; take heed and do it: for there is no iniquity with the LORD our God, nor respect of persons, nor taking of gifts" (2 Chronicles 19:6–7). He established in Jerusalem what was probably a court of appeals composed of Levites, priests, and chiefs of the fathers of Israel (2 Chronicles 19:8). To these he also gave a wholesome charge:

> Thus shall ye do in the fear of the LORD, faithfully, and with a perfect heart. And what cause soever shall come to you of your brethren that dwell in their cities, between blood and blood, between law and commandment, statutes and judgments, ye shall even warn them [that is, enlighten, teach, see Exodus 18:20] that they trespass not against the LORD, and so wrath come upon you, and upon your brethren: this do, and ye shall not trespass. And, behold, Amariah the chief priest is over you in all matters of the LORD; and Zebadiah the son of Ishmael, the ruler [prince] of the house of Judah, for all the king's matters: also the Levites shall be officers before you. Deal courageously, and the LORD shall be with the good (2 Chronicles 19:9–11).

"Matters of Jehovah" related to God's word or precepts; "the king's matters" to the civil things; and "controversies" were matters that came under the jurisdiction of the crown. "The Levites were to be *shorterim*, 'officers,' literally *scribes*, keeping written accounts; assistants to the judges, etc." (Fausset). All this would make for righteousness, and truly, "righteousness exalteth a nation," or any other body of people.

Satan could not stand idly by and witness this without making some attempt to disturb or destroy. "It came to pass after this also, that the children of Moab, and the children of Ammon, and with them other beside the Ammonites, came against Jehoshaphat to battle" (2 Chronicles 20:1). It was Satan, no doubt, who moved these neighboring nations to invade the land of Judah—whatever their motive may have been, whether jealousy, envy, greed, fear, or any other of the inciting causes of war among the nations of the earth. Scouts detected the movement and reported it to Jehoshaphat. "Then there came some that told Jehoshaphat, saying, There cometh a great multitude against thee from beyond the sea, on this side Syria; and, behold, they be in Hazezon-tamar, which is Engedi." They might well exclaim, "Behold," for Engedi was only twenty-five miles south of Jerusalem. The allies were almost upon them, "and Jehoshaphat feared." But though so nearly taken by surprise, the startling news did not create panic among the people. They were in communion with Jehovah. The king "set himself to seek the LORD, and proclaimed a fast throughout all Judah. And Judah gathered themselves together, to ask help of the LORD: even out of all the cities of Judah they came to seek the LORD" (3–4).

A great prayer meeting was held in the temple enclosure. The king himself prayed; and a most wonderful prayer it was (6–12).

> [Jehovah], God of our fathers, art not thou God in heaven? and rulest not thou over all the kingdoms of the heathen? and

in thine hand is there not power and might, so that none is able to withstand thee?...we stand before this house, and in thy presence (for thy name is in this house,) and cry unto thee in our affliction, then thou wilt hear and help....for we have no might against this great company that cometh against us; neither know we what to do: but our eyes are upon thee.

If they did not know what to do, they were then certainly doing the right thing when they cast themselves on God, and their expectation was from Him. "And all Judah stood before the LORD, with their little ones, their wives, and their children." Nor did He disappoint them.

> Then upon Jahaziel the son of Zechariah...a Levite of the sons of Asaph, came the Spirit of the LORD in the midst of the congregation; And he said, Hearken ye, all Judah...and thou, king Jehoshaphat, Thus saith the LORD unto you, Be not afraid nor dismayed by reason of this great multitude; for the battle is not yours, but God's....Ye shall not need to fight in this battle: set yourselves, stand ye still, and see the salvation of the LORD with you, O Judah and Jerusalem: fear not, nor be dismayed; to morrow go out against them: for the LORD will be with you (14–17).

How these words must have cheered the distressed king and his trembling people. "And Jehoshaphat bowed his head with his face to the ground: and all Judah and the inhabitants of Jerusalem fell before the LORD, worshipping the LORD." What a sight, to see the king and all his subjects bowed in worship before God for His promised mercy! And the prayer meeting became a praise meeting. "And the Levites, of the children of the Kohathites, and the children of the Korhites, stood up to praise the LORD God of Israel with a loud voice on high."

They rose early the next day, and as they went forth to meet the foe, Jehoshaphat said to them, "Believe in the LORD your God, so shall ye be established; believe his prophets, so shall ye prosper." He was not a haughty sovereign; for he consulted with his subjects. Then singers were appointed, and those that should praise in holy splendor, as they marched along at the head of the army, saying, "Praise the LORD; for his mercy endureth for ever." It is no longer prayer for deliverance, but thanksgiving for assured victory over the enemy.

> And when they began to sing and to praise, the LORD set ambushements against the children of Ammon, Moab, and mount Seir, which were come against Judah; and they were smitten. For the children of Ammon and Moab stood up against the inhabitants of mount Seir, utterly to slay and destroy them; and when they had made an end of the inhabitants of Seir, everyone helped to destroy another (22–23).

Never was a foreign invasion so easily repelled. An ambush set in some mysterious way by the Lord caused a panic among the allies, and they turned on one another to their mutual destruction. The deliverance came in a way altogether unexpected by Jehoshaphat, no doubt; but faith never asks how can or how will God fulfill His promise. It is enough to know that He *has promised;* the method must be left to Him.

> And when Judah came toward the watch tower in the wilderness, they looked unto the multitude, and, behold, they were dead bodies fallen to the earth, and none escaped. And when Jehoshaphat and his people came to take away the spoil of them, they found among them in abundance both riches with the dead bodies, and precious jewels, which they stripped off for themselves, more than they could carry away: and they

were three days in gathering of the spoil, it was so much (24–25).

And then, on the battlefield, they hold a thanksgiving meeting. "And on the fourth day they assembled themselves in the valley of Berachah; for there they blessed [Jehovah]: therefore the name of the same place was called, the valley of Berachah [blessing] unto this day." Fausset described this valley as "a broad, rich vale, watered with copious springs, affording space for a large multitude."

Psalm 48 is supposed to have been sung in the temple on their return to Jerusalem. "Then they returned, every man of Judah and Jerusalem, and Jehoshaphat in the forefront of them, to go again to Jerusalem with joy; for [Jehovah] had made them to rejoice over their enemies. And they came to Jerusalem with psalteries and harps and trumpets, unto the house of [Jehovah]."

This miraculous deliverance of Judah had a salutary effect on the nations around them. "And the fear of God was on all the kingdoms of those countries, when they had heard that [Jehovah] had fought against the enemies of Israel. So the realm of Jehoshaphat was quiet: for his God gave him rest round about" (2 Chronicles 20:29–30).

Jehoshaphat's alliance with the king of Israel and the king of Edom for the invasion of Moab was probably after this. It would be incomprehensible that a man of such piety and faith as Jehoshaphat possessed should be repeatedly betrayed into unholy confederacies if we did not know the weakness of the flesh. It is no better in the saint than in the sinner, and is ever ready to betray the saint into wrongdoing unless he watches against it in the spirit of humility and self-distrust. In both the Old and New Testaments, God's people are warned against the alliances of believers with unbelievers, of which

Jehoshaphat's history is a sad and solemn example. God had particularly forbidden and warned Israel against idolatry and intermarriages with the nations around, knowing full well how easily their weak heart would follow in the evil ways of the nations (see Deuteronomy 7:3–11; Exodus 20:4–5). In like manner, but in a more spiritual way, are we Christians exhorted and warned against all unequal yokes with unbelievers (see 2 Corinthians 6:11–18; 2 Timothy 2:20–21; 1 Peter 2:11–12; 1 John 2:15–17).

Jehoshaphat almost repeated his former alliance with Ahab. It will come before us again as we look at King Jehoram, so we do not stop to dwell on it here. These compromising entanglements appear to have been a special weakness with Jehoshaphat. He allied himself to Ahaziah, Ahab's son ("who did very wickedly"), to build ships to go to Tarshish. They were made at Ezion-geber where Solomon had his navy built (1 Kings 9:26). "Then Eliezer the son of Dodavah of Mareshah prophesied against Jehoshaphat, saying, Because thou hast joined thyself with Ahaziah, [Jehovah] hath broken thy works. And the ships were broken, that they were not able to go to Tarshish" (2 Chronicles 20:37). Psalm 48:7 seems to allude to this. Thus he linked himself during his reign with three kings of the wicked house of Ahab, to his humiliation and sorrow; first with Ahab himself, and then with his sons Ahaziah and Joram or Jehoram. No good came of any of these associations. The ships built in partnership were hardly launched before they were broken at *Ezion-geber*—"the devils backbone" (Fausset) (1 Kings 22:48). There is always something of the wiles or power of Satan in these unequal yokes. Child of God, beware of them!

Jehoshaphat reigned twenty-five years, and died at the age of sixty. His mother, Azubah, was the single Scripture namesake of Caleb's first wife (1 Chronicles 2:18).

JEHORAM

Exalted by Jehovah
(1 Kings 22:50; 2 Kings 8:16–24; 2 Chronicles 21)

Give not thy . . . ways to that which destroyeth kings.

Proverbs 31:3

Of the seven sons of Jehoshaphat, Jehoram was the oldest, and his father gave him the kingdom. It would seem, from 2 Kings 8:16, that he associated Jehoram with him on the throne during his lifetime. Jehoshaphat probably foresaw and feared what was likely to occur after his death; to avert, if possible, any such disaster, he endeavored to have the throne well secured to Jehoram before his decease. To conciliate his remaining six sons, he "gave them great gifts of silver, and of gold, and of precious things, with fenced cities in Judah" (2 Chronicles 21:3). They were not, probably, all children of one mother, as two of them bear exactly the same name—Azariah. This would make dissension among them all the more likely, and it is a warning to all to see Jehoshaphat ending his days with this threatening storm cloud hanging over his house.

The chaos and evil of Jehoshaphat's reign was the result of his ill-advised alliance with the ungodly house of Ahab, and what he sowed he, by dread anticipation at least, reaped. Actually his posterity were made to reap it in a most terrible way. "Now when Jehoram was risen up to the kingdom of his father, he strengthened himself, and slew all his brethren with the sword, and divers also of the princes of Israel" (21:4). He had married the daughter of a "murderer" (2 Kings 6:32), and as a natural consequence he soon soaked his own hands in blood. "Jehoram was thirty and two years old when he began to reign, and he reigned eight years in Jerusalem. And he walked in the ways of the kings of Israel, like as did the house of Ahab: for he had the daughter of Ahab to wife: and he wrought that which was evil in the eyes of the LORD" (2 Chronicles 21:5–6).

Decadence of power at once set in, which the neighboring nations were quick to perceive and take advantage of. "In his days the Edomites revolted from under the dominion of Judah, and made themselves a king. Then Jehoram went forth with his princes, and all his chariots with him: and he rose up by night, and smote the Edomites which compassed him in, and the captains of the chariots" (8–9). This happened at Zair (2 Kings 8:21), in Idumea, south of the Dead Sea. He barely escaped destruction or capture, being surrounded by the enemy. He managed to extricate himself by a night surprise, but the expedition was a failure. "So the Edomites revolted from under the hand of Judah unto this day" (2 Chronicles 21:10). The spirit of rebellion spread: "The same time also did Libnah revolt from under his hand; because he had forsaken the LORD God of his fathers."

Jehoram

His attitude toward idolatry was the exact reverse of that of his father. "He made high places in the mountains of Judah, and caused the inhabitants of Jerusalem to commit fornication, and compelled Judah thereto," or, "seduced Judah." He undid, so far as lay in his power, all the good work of his father Jehoshaphat. But how dearly he paid for his wickedness!

> And there came a writing to him from Elijah the prophet [evidently written prophetically before his translation], saying, Thus saith the LORD God of David thy father, Because thou hast not walked in the ways of Jehoshaphat thy father, nor in the ways of Asa king of Judah, but hast walked in the way of the kings of Israel, and hast made Judah and the inhabitants of Jerusalem to go a whoring, like to the whoredoms of the house of Ahab, and also hast slain thy brethren of thy father's house, which were better than thyself: Behold, with a great plague will the LORD smite thy people, and thy children, and thy wives, and all thy goods: And thou shalt have great sickness by disease of thy bowels, until thy bowels fall out by reason of the sickness day by day (12–15).

Elijah's ministry and field of labor had been, it would seem, exclusively among the ten tribes, the kingdom of Israel. But the servant of God is used here for a message to the king of Judah. And as it was prophesied to him, so it came to pass.

> The LORD stirred up against Jehoram the spirit of the Philistines, and of the Arabians, that were near the Ethiopians: And they came up into Judah, and brake into it, and carried away all the substance that was found in the king's house, and his sons also, and his wives; so that there was never a son left him, save Jehoahaz [called Ahaziah in 2 Chronicles 22:1], the

youngest of his sons. And after all this [terrible as the stroke was] the LORD smote him in his bowels with an incurable disease. And it came to pass, that in process of time, after the end of two years, his bowels fell out by reason of his sickness: so he died of sore diseases. And his people made no burning for him, like the burning of his fathers (16–19).

What a terrible recompense for his murders and idolatries! God made a signal example of him, that his successors might "see it and fear."

"Thirty and two years old was he when he began to reign, and he reigned in Jerusalem eight years, and departed without being desired [regretted]. Howbeit they buried him in the city of David, but not in the sepulchres of the kings." He is one of the most unlovely of all the kings of Judah. Although his name means "exalted by Jehovah," he was for his wickedness thrust down to a dishonored grave. He took the kingdom when raised to its highest glory since the days of Solomon, and left it, after a reign of eight short years, with *Ichabod* ("the glory is departed") written large upon it.

The proverb, "One sinner destroyeth much good" (Ecclesiastes 9:18), was sadly exemplified in this unhappy Jehoram's life. The lifetime's labor of a devoted man of God may be easily and quickly ruined or marred by some such sinner. We see this illustrated in the case of Paul. After his departure, "grievous wolves" entered in among the flocks gathered by his toils and travail. Also men arose among them, "speaking perverse things, to draw away the disciples after them" (Acts 20:29–30). And even before his martyrdom he wrote, weeping, of "the enemies of the cross of Christ," and was compelled to say, "All seek their own, not the things which are Jesus Christ's." Also, "All they which be in Asia are turned away from me." And one has only to compare the writings of the earliest Greek fathers with the writings of the apostle, to see how widespread and complete was the departure from the truth of Christianity. "Nevertheless [blessed word!] the foundation of God standeth sure." "And," the exhortation is, "let every one that nameth the name of the Lord depart from iniquity" (2 Timothy 2:19). Oh, let not *me* be the sinner to "destroy the work of God" (Romans 14:20).

AHAZIAH
(Jehoahaz or Azariah)

Sustained by Jehovah
(2 Kings 8:24–27; 9:27–29; 2 Chronicles 22:1–9)

For, lo, the kings were assembled, they passed by together.
                                                    Psalm 48:4

*A*haziah must have reigned as his father's viceroy during the last year of the latter's sickness. This is evident from a comparison of 2 Kings 8:25 with 9:29. He was the youngest and only remaining son of Jehoram (2 Chronicles 21:17). "Two and twenty years old was Ahaziah when he began to reign." ("Forty and two" in 2 Chronicles 22:2 is doubtless a transcriber's error. His father was only forty at his death.) "And he reigned one year in Jerusalem. And his mother's name was Athaliah, the daughter [or granddaughter] of Omri king of Israel. And he walked in the way of the house of Ahab, and did evil in the sight of the Lord, as did the house of Ahab: for he was the son in law of the house of Ahab" (2 Kings 8:26–27). His mother, in some way or other, escaped the fate of the rest of Jehoram's wives (who were carried away captive at the time of the Philistine-Arabian invasion), and "was his counsellor to do wickedly."

Second Chronicles 22:4 seems to give a slight hint that his father Jehoram repented during his last sufferings, and had broken away somewhat from the house of Ahab; "for they were his [Ahaziah's] counsellors after the death of his father to his destruction." His father's death removed the check, and he at once united himself with his mother's relatives in their sins and warfare. "He walked also after their counsel, and went with Jehoram the son of Ahab king of Israel to war against Hazael king of Syria at Ramoth-gilead."

This friendship cost him his life.

> And the Syrians smote Joram [the king of Israel]. And he returned to be healed in Jezreel because of the wounds which were given him in Ramah [or Ramoth], when he fought with Hazael king of Syria. And Azariah [Ahaziah] the son of Jehoram king of Judah went down to see Jehoram the son of Ahab at Jezreel, because he was sick. And the destruction of Ahaziah was of God by coming to Joram: for when he was come, he went out with Jehoram against Jehu the son of Nimshi, whom the LORD had anointed to cut off the house of Ahab (2 Chronicles 22:5–7).

Ahaziah saw his uncle Jehoram slain in his chariot, and tried in vain to make his escape from the hot-headed Jehu. "He fled by the way of the garden house. And Jehu followed after him, and said, Smite him also in the chariot. And they did so at the going up to Gur, which is by Ibleam. And he fled to Megiddo, and died there. And his servants carried him in a chariot to Jerusalem, and buried him in his sepulchre with his fathers in the city of David" (2 Kings 9:27–28). The account in Chronicles says, "he was hid in Samaria." There is no discrepancy here, for when he fled to the garden house (Bethzan), he escaped to Samaria (or the kingdom of Samaria) where were his "brethren" and the princes of Judah. Thence, followed by Jehu, he was pursued to the hill Gur, and slain. "And when they had slain him, they buried him: Because, said they, he is the son of Jehoshaphat, who sought the LORD with all his heart" (2 Chronicles 22:9). His being the grandson of Jehoshaphat was all that saved his body from being eaten by unclean dogs, like the bodies of his great-aunt Jezebel and her son Jehoram.

"So the house of Ahaziah had no power to keep still the kingdom." And with these cheerless words the record of the reign of Ahaziah closes. He was the seventh from Solomon, and the first king of Judah to die a violent death. His name is the first of the royal line omitted in the genealogy of Matthew 1. The first of the three names given him, Jehoahaz—"whom Jehovah helps"—is markedly at variance with his character. This may be the reason why he is called by that name only once in Scripture (2 Chronicles 21:17).

He died at the early age of twenty-three. It was not part of Jehu's commission to slay the king of Judah, but he was found among those doomed to destruction and consequently shared their fate. And God's call to His own in that system of iniquity where the spiritual Jezebel teaches and seduces His servants is, "Come out of her, my people, that ye be not partakers of her sins, *and that ye receive not of her plagues*" (Revelation 18:4, italics added). Oh that all God's people might even now lay this call to heart, and separate themselves from that which is fast shaping itself for its ultimate apostasy and doom!

JEHOASH
(or Joash)

Jehovah-gifted
(2 Kings 11–12; 2 Chronicles 22:10–24:27)

CONTEMPORARY PROPHET: Zechariah, son of Jehoiada

It is he that giveth salvation unto kings: who delivereth David his servant from the hurtful sword.

Psalm 144:10

And when Athaliah the mother of Ahaziah saw that her son was dead, she arose and destroyed all the seed royal. [Chronicles adds, "of the house of Judah."] But Jehosheba, the daughter of king Joram, sister of Ahaziah, took Joash the son of Ahaziah, and stole him from among the king's sons which were slain; and they hid him, even him and his nurse, in the bedchamber from Athaliah, so that he was not slain" (2 Kings 11:1–2).

Second Chronicles 24:7 describes Athaliah as "That wicked woman." She was just such a daughter as her infamous mother, Jezebel, was likely to produce. Her father was himself a murderer, and the family character was fully marked in her. She heartlessly slaughtered her own grandchildren in her lust for power. She herself would be ruler of the kingdom, even at the cost of the lives of helpless and innocent children. No character in history, sacred or secular, stands out blacker or more hideous than this daughter-in-law of the godly Jehoshaphat.

Joash was only an infant at the time, and his mother (Zibiah of Beersheba) was in all likelihood dead—probably murdered by her fiendish mother-in-law. Jehosheba ("Jehovah's oath", that is, devoted to Him), the child's aunt and wife of the high priest Jehoiada ("Jehovah known"), hid Joash and his nurse, first in one of the palace bedchambers, and later in the temple (where she lived) among her own children and perhaps as one of them. "And he was with them hid in the house of God six years: and Athaliah reigned over the land" (2 Chronicles 22:12). Through this, God displayed his mercy to the house of David, even as it had been declared at the time of the reign of Athaliah's husband Jehoram: "Howbeit the LORD would not destroy the house of David, because of the covenant that he had made with David, and as he promised to give a light to him and to his sons for ever" (2 Chronicles 21:7).

Athaliah, no doubt, thought herself secure on the throne of David. Six years she possessed the coveted power, and could say, "I sit a queen." She made the most of her opportunity to corrupt the kingdom with idolatry, and had a temple built to Baal. But in the seventh year her richly-merited retribution suddenly came upon her.

Jehoash

And the seventh year Jehoiada sent and fetched the rulers over hundreds, with the captains and the guard, and brought them to him into the house of the LORD, and made a covenant with them, and took an oath of them in the house of the LORD, and showed them the king's son (2 Kings 11:4). And they went about in Judah, and gathered the Levites out of all the cities of Judah, and the chief of the fathers of Israel, and they came to Jerusalem. And all the congregation made a covenant with the king in the house of God. And he [Jehoiada] said unto them, Behold, the king's son shall reign, as the LORD hath said of the sons of David (2 Chronicles 23:2–3).

Arrangements were then entered into for the most unique coronation that was ever known. Everything was ordered with great care and secrecy so that suspicion would not be aroused. Trusted men, chiefly Levites, were stationed at important points about the king's house and temple. The Sabbath day, and the time for the changing of the courses of the priests and Levites, may have been chosen so that the unusually large number of people about the temple would not excite suspicion in the minds of Athaliah and her Baalite minions. The Levites carefully guarded the royal child, "every man with his weapons in his hand," with strict orders to slay any one that would attempt to approach him. "And to the captains over hundreds did the priest give king David's spears and shields, that were in the temple of the LORD," and a strong guard was placed within the temple enclosure. "Then they brought out the king's son, and put upon him the crown, and gave him the testimony [a copy of the law, Deuteronomy 17:18], and made him king. Jehoiada and his sons anointed him, and said, God save the king!" It is a thrilling tale, and nowhere given so well as in our time-honored King James version.

"Now when Athaliah heard the noise of the people running and praising the king, she came to the people into the house of the LORD: and she looked, and, behold, the king stood at [or, on] his pillar [*Gesenius* "stage" or "scaffold"] at the entering in, and the princes and the trumpets by the king: and all the people of the land rejoiced, and sounded with trumpets, also the singers with instruments of music, and such as taught to sing praise. Then Athaliah rent her clothes, and said, Treason, Treason" (2 Chronicles 23:12–13).

> But Jehoiada the priest commanded the captains of the hundreds, the officers of the host, and said unto them, Have her forth without the ranges: and him that followeth her kill with the sword.…And Jehoiada made a covenant between the LORD and the king and the people, that they should be the LORD's people; between the king also and the people. And all the people of the land went into the house of Baal, and brake it down; his altars and his images brake they in pieces thoroughly, and slew Mattan the priest of Baal before the altars.…and they brought down the king from the house of the LORD, and came by the way of the gate of the guard to the king's house. And he sat on the throne of the kings. And all the people of the land rejoiced, and the city was in quiet: and they slew Athaliah with the sword beside the king's house (2 Kings 11:15–20).

Jehoiada and his wife had engaged in this dangerous business in faith, as is evident by the words of Jehoiada, "Behold the king's son shall reign, as the LORD hath said of the sons of David." "The Lord hath said" is quite enough for faith to act on whatever be the dangers, the difficulties, and the toils. And in that path of obedience all the wheels of providence are made to turn to bring about the successful end. God gives the needful wisdom in it too, and so every step and arrangement

Jehoash

of faithful Jehoiada succeeds perfectly, all proving that whatever be the cunning and craft of the devil in Athaliah, it must succumb to the wisdom of God and of faith. The cause was of God; Joash was the only rightful heir to the throne of David, which by the promise of God was not to be without an heir till that Heir should come who would be "the sure mercies of David" and would need no successor.

> Joash was seven years old when he began to reign, and he reigned forty years in Jerusalem. His mother's name also was Zibiah ["doe" or "gazelle"] of Beersheba. And Joash did that which was right in the sight of the LORD all the days of Jehoiada the priest. And Jehoiada took for him two wives; and he begat sons and daughters (2 Chronicles 24:1–3).

His uncle appears to have exercised a wholesome influence over him. The noting of his taking two wives for him is doubtless to manifest his godly concern for the succession of the line of David.

"And it came to pass after this, that Joash was minded to repair the house of the LORD. And he gathered together the priests and the Levites, and said to them, Go out into the cities of Judah, and gather of all Israel money to repair the house of your God from year to year, and see that ye hasten the matter. Howbeit the Levites hastened it not" (4–5). Nothing was done at the time. The spiritual condition of the people made it difficult to accomplish anything. "The people still sacrificed and burnt incense in the high places," and would therefore feel little responsibility toward the temple at Jerusalem. The lines in Pope's pantheistic poem, "The Universal Prayer" would, no doubt, express pretty accurately the thoughts of the Israelites regarding the worship of God: "To Thee whose temple is all space, / Whose altar, earth, sea, skies!"

The money that was contributed was, it would seem, misappropriated towards the maintenance of the priests and Levites (see 2 Kings 12:7–8). This neglect continued until the twenty-third year of Joash.

> And the king called for Jehoiada the chief, and said unto him, Why hast thou not required of the Levites to bring in out of Judah and out of Jerusalem the collection, according to the commandment of Moses the servant of the LORD, and of the congregation of Israel, for the tabernacle of witness? [Evidently he had not neglected to read the "testimony" delivered to him at his coronation.] For the sons of Athaliah, that wicked woman, had broken up the house of God; and also all the dedicated things of the house of the LORD did they bestow upon Baalim (2 Chronicles 24:6–7).

True to what he had learned in the Word of God, Joash did not hesitate to admonish even the high priest if he was negligent in obeying it, for that Word is above all. And though he owed to his uncle a lasting debt of gratitude for the preservation of his infant life, he could, when occasion required, request that as God's high priest Jehoiada perform his duty in reference to the necessary repairs of that house over which he had been set by God. Would God that Joash had continued in such a mind to the end of his reign.

> And at the king's commandment they made a chest, and set it without at the gate of the house of the LORD. And they made a proclamation through Judah and Jerusalem, to bring in to the LORD the collection that Moses the servant of God laid upon Israel in the wilderness [see Exodus 30:11–16]. And all the princes and all the people rejoiced, and brought in, and cast into the chest, until they had made an end (8–10).

Jehoash

The people's conscience was stirred, and they gave as the Lord loves to see His people give—cheerfully. No exacting accounts were kept; there was no suspicion of dishonesty, or misappropriation; the most beautiful confidence prevailed, evidencing the work of God (11–13). When God's work is being done, the heart is engaged; selfish ends are absent; there is one common object; all this produces confidence: "Moreover they reckoned not with the men, into whose hand they delivered the money to be bestowed on the workmen: for they dealt faithfully" (2 Kings 12:15).

More than sufficient was bestowed by the willing-hearted people. "And when they had finished it, they brought the rest of the money before the king and Jehoiada, whereof were made vessels for the house of the LORD, even vessels to minister, and to offer withal, and spoons, and vessels of gold and silver" (2 Chronicles 24:14). Nor were the priests left unprovided for. "The trespass money and sin money was not brought into the house of [Jehovah]: it was the priest's" (2 Kings 12:16).

> And they offered burnt offerings in the house of the LORD continually all the days of Jehoiada. But Jehoiada waxed old, and was full of days when he died; an hundred and thirty years old was he when he died. And they buried him in the city of David among the kings [as well they might], because he had done good in Israel, both toward God, and toward his house (2 Chronicles 24:14–16).

He had remembered the claims of the holy One of Israel, and attended to them with vigor and fidelity. Nor could it be other than the energy of faith in a man nearly a hundred years old setting himself to overthrow such an enemy of God as Athaliah.

His extreme old age may account for his evident laxity in

performing the king's command in regard to the repairing of the temple. He was born before the death of Solomon, and had seen much during his long life that peculiarly qualified him to become the protector and early guide of Jehoash. By him the kingdom was reestablished, and the cause of Jehovah revived during his last days on earth. He was a true king, in heart and mind, and it was appropriate that the aged patriarch's mitered head should be laid to rest among those who had worn the crown.

How long he had filled the office of high priest is not known. He succeeded Amariah, who was high priest under Jehoshaphat. What a contrast between him and those other two high priests, Annas and Caiaphas, of whom we read in the New Testament. He labored to maintain the succession; they labored to destroy the final Heir—"great David's greater son." And when the time of rewards comes, what will be the unspeakable differences!

But now a cloud begins to appear that dims the brightness of the reign of Joash, and culminates in treachery and murder.

> Now after the death of Jehoiada came the princes of Judah, and made obeisance to the king. Then the king hearkened unto them. And they left the house of the LORD God of their fathers, and served groves and idols: and wrath came upon Judah and Jerusalem for this their trespass. Yet He sent prophets to them, to bring them again unto the LORD; and they testified against them: but they would not give ear (2 Chronicles 24:17–19).

The revival during Joash's early reign had already lost its hold. It could not have been of much depth when they could so quickly turn aside to idols after Jehoiada's departure. But

Jehoash

the spirit of the good high priest was not dead; his worthy son Zechariah withstood and condemned their backslidings.

> And the Spirit of God came upon Zechariah the son of Jehoiada the priest, which stood above the people, and said unto them, Thus saith God, Why transgress ye the commandments of the LORD, that ye cannot prosper? because ye have forsaken the LORD, he hath also forsaken you. And they conspired against him, and stoned him with stones at the commandment of the king, in the court of the house of the LORD (2 Chronicles 24:20–21).

"At the commandment of the king"! Alas for Joash's unfaithfulness to God, and base ingratitude to the man who had been to him so great a benefactor! Zechariah was his cousin, and his foster brother too! "Thus Joash the king remembered not the kindness which Jehoiada his father had done to him, but slew his son. And when he died, he said, The LORD look upon it, and require it" (22). This is, in all probability, the *Zacharias* referred to by our Lord: "That upon you may come all the righteous blood shed upon the earth, from the blood of righteous Abel unto the blood of Zacharias son of Barachias, whom ye slew, between the temple and the altar" (Matthew 23:35). He was the last *historical* Old Testament martyr, as Abel had been the first. The prophet Urijah was slain almost two hundred and fifty years after Zechariah, but it is not recorded in the historical canon of Scripture; it is only mentioned incidentally in Jeremiah 26:23. "Son of Barachias" presents no real difficulty. It may have been a second name for Jehoiada (and would be a very appropriate one too as *Barachias* means "blessed"); or, Barachias may have been one of Zechariah's earlier ancestors, as "son of" frequently means in Scripture. Luke 11:51 does not have "son of Barachias." But one of the first of the above explanations is preferable. Anyway, he met his death at the hand of the very man for whom his mother and his father risked their lives. Other sons of Jehoiada were also slain by Joash (2 Chronicles 24:25). "The LORD look upon it, and require it," the dying martyr said. Stephen, also stoned for his testimony, cried, "Lord, lay not this sin to their charge." Law, under which "every transgression and disobedience received a just recompense of reward," was the governing principle of the dispensation under which the martyr Zechariah died, whereas grace reigned in Stephen's day (as still in ours); therefore the difference in the dying martyrs' prayers. Both, though so unalike, were in perfect keeping with the dispensations under which they witnessed.

"The LORD require it." And He did, and swiftly—for He does not disregard the dying prayers of men like Zechariah.

> And it came to pass at the end of the year, that the host of Syria came up against him: and they came to Judah and Jerusalem, and destroyed all the princes of the people from among the people and sent all the spoil of them unto the king of Damascus. For the army of the Syrians came with a small company of men, and the LORD delivered a very great host into their hand, because they had forsaken the LORD God of their fathers. So they executed judgment against Joash. And when they were departed from him (for they left him in great diseases), his own servants conspired against him for the blood of the sons of Jehoiada the priest, and slew him on his bed, and he died: and they buried him in the city of David, but they buried him not in the sepulchres of the kings (2 Chronicles 24:23–25).

The princes were judged first for they held the largest responsibility for persuading the king to forsake Jehovah.

Jehoash

Second Kings 12:17–18 records a previous invasion of Syrians under Hazael, when Joash bought him off with gold and other treasures taken from the temple and the king's palace. It was then that they discovered the real weakness of the army of Joash (in spite of its being "a very great host"); hence only "a small company of men" was sent out on the second expedition against him.

"There is no king saved by the multitude of an host," (Psalm 33:16) wrote that king whose throne Joash so unworthily filled. His time to receive the due reward of his deeds was come, and there was no power on earth that could have saved him. The murdered Zechariah's name (meaning "Jah hath remembered") must have had a terrible significance to him as he lay in "great diseases" on his bed in the house of Millo, the citadel of Zion. And if he escaped death at the hands of the Syrians by taking refuge in the stronghold at the descent of Silla (2 Kings 12:20), it was only to be treacherously assassinated by his servants. Both of them were sons of Gentile women (2 Chronicles 24:26), fruit of mixed marriages, condemned by the law. So disobedience brings its own bitter reward, and what God's people sow they always, in some way or other, reap. Joash abundantly deserved his inglorious and terrible end. It can always be said, when the judgments of God are seen to come on such as he: "Thou art righteous, O Lord, which art, and wast, and shalt be, because thou hast judged thus. For they have shed the blood of saints and prophets, and thou hast given them blood to drink; for they are worthy" (Revelation 16:5–6).

AMAZIAH

Strength of Jah
(2 Kings 14:1–20; 2 Chronicles 25)

CONTEMPORARY PROPHETS: Several unnamed (two in 2 Chronicles 25)

A king ready to the battle.

Job 15:24

Amaziah was twenty and five years old when he began to reign, and he reigned twenty and nine years in Jerusalem. And his mother's name was Jehoaddan ['Jehovah-pleased'] of Jerusalem." He evidently reigned a year jointly with his father (compare 2 Kings 13:10; 14:1; 2 Chronicles 24:1) during the latter's last sickness, when the "great diseases" were upon him.

"And he did that which was right in the sight of the LORD, but not with a perfect heart" (2 Chronicles 25:2). "Yet not like David his father," it is said; "he did according to all things as Joash his father did" (2 Kings 14:3). This exemplifies the lack of heart devotedness in some of God's children. He allowed the high places to remain, and the people sacrificed and burned incense on them.

> Now it came to pass, when the kingdom was established to him, that he slew his servants that had killed the king his father. But he slew not their children, but did as it is written in the law, in the book of Moses, where the LORD commanded, saying, The fathers shall not die for the children, neither shall the children die for the fathers, but every man shall die for his own sin (2 Chronicles 25:3–4).

He made a good beginning in thus adhering closely to the law (see Deuteronomy 24:16). Happy would it have been for him and for his kingdom had he continued as he began. "As soon as the kingdom was confirmed in his hand" (2 Kings 14:5) appears to imply that the state affairs were somewhat unsettled at his father's death. What follows confirms this thought. "Moreover Amaziah gathered Judah together, and made them captains over thousands, and captains over hundreds, according to the houses of their fathers, throughout all Judah and Benjamin." He began to reorganize the scattered army. "And he numbered them from twenty years old and above, and found them three hundred thousand choice men, able to go forth to war, that could handle spear and shield."

An expedition against Edom was probably in his mind in this organization of his forces. And trusting the multitude of a host more than the Lord, "he hired also a hundred thousand

Amaziah

mighty men of valor out of Israel for an hundred talents of silver." But God does not want mercenaries in His battles—neither then, nor now. So "there came a man of God to him, saying, O king, let not the army of Israel go with thee; for the LORD is not with Israel, to wit, with all the children of Ephraim. But if thou wilt go [with them], do it, be strong for the battle: God shall make thee fall before the enemy: for," he added, "God hath power to help, and to cast down" (2 Chronicles 25:7–8). He may retain them if he wished, but he has the consequences set before him. God knew the corrupting influence this body of Ephraimites would have on the army of Judah. "Shouldest thou help the ungodly?" the prophet Jehu asked Jehoshaphat. In this case Amaziah reversed the order, and would have the ungodly help him. And, besides, the children of Ephraim were not particularly famous for their courage. "The children of Ephraim, being armed, and carrying bows, turned back in the day of battle," was their inglorious record (Psalm 78:9). But Amaziah thinks of the advance wages already paid to these hireling warriors: "But what shall we do for the hundred talents which I have given to the army [literally, troop or band] of Israel? And the man of God answered, The LORD is able to give thee much more than this" (9). This is a good exhortation for any child of God who may find himself in a position compromising the truth, and who cannot see his way out without serious financial loss. "The Lord is able to give thee much more than this"; and if He does not more than make it up in temporal things, He will repay it in what is infinitely better—in those spiritual things, which are eternal. "To obey is better than sacrifice," anyway and always.

Amaziah considered the prophet's advice and separated the mercenaries, and sent them home again. "Wherefore their anger was greatly kindled against Judah, and they returned home in great [fierce] anger." This refusal of their assistance only revealed their real character. They had long ago turned away from Jehovah; what did they care now for His honor or the good of Judah? So they avenged their supposed insult by falling upon defenseless cities on Judah's northern frontier. They plundered them, and mercilessly slaughtered three thousand of their own flesh and blood. Such men could not help in God's army then; neither can men with selfish motives be helpful in Christ's cause now.

> And Amaziah strengthened himself, and led forth his people, and went to the valley of salt [south of the Dead Sea], and smote of the children of Seir ten thousand. And other ten thousand left alive did the children of Judah carry away captive, and brought them unto the top of the rock, and cast them down from the top of the rock, that they all were broken in pieces (2 Chronicles 25:11–12).

This seemingly cruel treatment of conquered enemies is related without comment. We know nothing of the attendant circumstances, nor the cause of Judah's invasion. They lived in the cold, hard age of law ("eye for eye, tooth for tooth, nail for nail"), and we must not measure their conduct by the standard we have received from Him who came not to destroy men's lives, but to save them. During the eighteenth century men were hung in enlightened "Christian" England for stealing sheep. Voltaire seems never to have condemned the English for it. Yet what government, for a like offense, would take a human life today? Amaziah's army may have believed themselves justified in meting out such horrible punishment to the Edomites. But we neither judge nor excuse them for their terrible act. God has left it without comment. It was not God's act, but Amaziah's.

He "took Selah [or *Petra*, "the rock," Edom's capital] by

Amaziah

war, and called the name of it Joktheel unto this day" (2 Kings 14:7). "It lay in a hollow, enclosed amidst cliffs, and accessible only by a ravine through which the river winds across its site" (Fausset). *Joktheel* means "the reward of God" so Amaziah seems to have looked at this captured city as God's repayment for the one hundred silver talents lost on the worthless Ephraimites. And does not God ever repay His obedient people with abundant increase?

But success with Amaziah (as with most of us) puffed him up. Inflated with his subjugation of the Edomites, he impudently challenged the king of Israel to meet him in combat, saying, "Come, let us look one another in the face" (8). The offended Ephraimites had indeed wantonly wronged some of his subjects; yet for this the king of Israel was less responsible than Amaziah himself, who had hired them to enter his army. In Chronicles 25:17 we read that he "took advice" in challenging the king of Israel. Like his father Joash, he was led into disaster by the counsel of the ungodly. But it was of God, for the punishment of his idolatry. For, before this we read:

> After that Amaziah was come from the slaughter of the Edomites, that he brought the gods of the children of Seir, and set them up to be his gods, and bowed down himself before them, and burned incense unto them. Wherefore the anger of the LORD was kindled against Amaziah, and he sent unto him a prophet, which said unto him, Why hast thou sought after the gods of the people, which could not deliver their own people out of thy hand? [A child might understand such reasoning.] And it came to pass, as he talked with him, that the king said unto him, Art thou made of the king's counsel? forbear; why shouldest thou be smitten? Then the prophet forbare, and said, I know that God hath determined to destroy thee, because

thou hast done this, and hast not hearkened unto my counsel (2 Chronicles 25:14–16).

So God let him take other counsel (since he refused His own), that led to his ruin.

To Amaziah's rash challenge the king of Israel made a scornful reply by the language of a parable. He said:

> The thistle that was in Lebanon [Amaziah] sent to the cedar that was in Lebanon [Joash], saying, Give thy daughter to my son to wife: and there passed by a wild beast that was in Lebanon [Joash's army], and trod down the thistle. [And he adds,] Thou sayest [to thyself], Lo, thou hast smitten the Edomites; and thine heart lifteth thee up to boast: abide now at home; why shouldest thou meddle to thine hurt, that thou shouldest fall, even thou, and Judah with thee? [This is good, sound advice.] But Amaziah would not hear; for it came of God, that he might deliver them into the hand of their enemies, because they sought after the gods of Edom.... And Judah was put to the worse before Israel, and they fled every man to his tent. And Joash the king of Israel took Amaziah king of Judah...and brought him to Jerusalem, and brake down the wall of Jerusalem from the gate of Ephraim to the corner gate, four hundred cubits (18–23).

This is the first time the walls of Jerusalem had ever been injured. It was on the north—the only side from which the city is easily accessible. Josephus stated that Joash gained entrance into the city by threatening to kill their captive king if the inhabitants refused to open the gates. The victorious Joash, king of Israel, took all the gold and silver and the holy vessels, and all the treasures that were found in the temple and the king's house; he took hostages also, and returned to Samaria.

Amaziah

Amaziah lived more than fifteen years after his humiliating defeat and capture by the king of Israel. He died by violence, like his father and grandfather before him. "Now after the time that Amaziah did turn away from following the LORD they made a conspiracy against him in Jerusalem; and he fled to Lachish: but they sent to Lachish after him, and slew him there. And they brought him upon horses, and buried him with his fathers in the city of Judah" or of David (27–28). His "turning away from following the LORD" was probably his final and complete apostasy from Jehovah God of Israel; not when he first bowed down to the gods of Seir, which was the beginning of his downward course.

Lachish was the first of the cities of Judah to adopt the idolatries of the kingdom of Israel—"she is the beginning of the sin to the daughter of Zion: for the transgressions of Israel were found in thee" (Micah 1:13)—and it was natural for the idolatrous Amaziah to seek an asylum there. They brought his body back to Jerusalem on horses, as they would a beast (contrast Acts 7:16). His name means "strength of Jah," but we read, "he strengthened himself" (2 Chronicles 25:11). His character of self-sufficiency belied his name—a thing not uncommon in our day, *especially among a people called "Christians."*

He was assassinated at the age of fifty-four. His mother's name, "Jehovah-pleased," would indicate that she was a woman of piety. It may be that it was due to her influence that he acted righteously during the earlier portion of his reign. The record of his reign has the same sad monotony of so many of the kings of Judah at this period—"his acts first and last"—the first, full of promise; and the last, declension or apostasy. "Wherefore let him that thinketh he standeth take heed lest he fall" (1 Corinthians 10:12).

UZZIAH
(or Azariah)

Strength of Jehovah
(2 Kings 15:1–7; 2 Chronicles 26)

CONTEMPORARY PROPHETS: Zechariah of 2 Chronicles 26:5, Isaiah, Hosea, and Amos

He [the Lord] shall cut off the spirit of princes: he is terrible to the kings of the earth.

Psalm 76:12

When all the people of Judah took Uzziah, who was sixteen years old, and made him king in the room of his father Amaziah. He built Eloth, and restored it to Judah, after that the king slept with his fathers" (2 Chronicles 26:1–2). He is called Azariah ("helped by Jehovah") elsewhere; the names were so nearly equivalent in meaning as to be applied

KINGS OF JUDAH

interchangeably to him. He seems to have come by the throne, not in the way of ordinary succession, but by the direct choice of the people. The princes had been destroyed by the Syrians toward the close of his grandfather Joash's reign (2 Chronicles 24:23), leaving the people a free hand. "For the transgression of a land many are the princes thereof," wrote Solomon, more than a century before. This weeding out was not altogether to be regretted and perhaps not entirely unnecessary. If the princes selfishly "seek their own" things, they are incapable of judging aright; while a needy, suffering people instinctively turn to a deliverer. Their choice here of Azariah was a good one, as the sequel proved.

His first recorded work, the building, enlargement, or fortification of Eloth (Elath), and its restoration to the crown of Judah, was an early pledge of the great industrial prosperity of his reign. It belonged to Edom, and was lost to Judah during the reign of Joram (2 Kings 8:20). It was a seaport on the Red Sea, near Ezion-geber (1 Kings 9:26), and must have made a most important market for the extensive commerce in his administration. Fifty years later it was taken by Rezin king of Syria, who expelled the Jews and occupied it permanently (see 2 Kings 16:6).

"Sixteen years old was Uzziah when he began to reign, and he reigned fifty and two years in Jerusalem. His mother's name also was Jecoliah of Jerusalem." His was the longest continuous reign of any of the kings of Judah. Manasseh's reign of fifty-five years was interrupted by his deposition and captivity by the king of Babylon. His mother's name, "Jah will enable," might indicate that she had pious expectations of her son, by the help of God. And in this she would not be disappointed, for "he did that which was right in the sight of the LORD, according to all that his father Amaziah did"—that is, during the earlier portion of Amaziah's reign. "And he

Uzziah

sought God in the days of Zechariah, who had understanding in the visions of God: and as long as he sought the LORD, God made him to prosper." "Understanding in the visions of God" is not equivalent to having prophetical visions from God. The Septuagint and other early manuscripts read, "who was (his) instructor in the fear of God," which is probably the general sense of the expression. Nothing more is known of this prophet, but his record is on high, and the coming day will declare what else, whether of good or bad, was accomplished by him during his earthly life.

From city building for the peaceful purpose of commerce, Uzziah turns to retributive warfare. "And he went forth and warred against the Philistines, and brake down the wall of Gath, and the wall of Jabneh, and the wall of Ashdod, and built cities about [or, in the country of] Ashdod and among the Philistines. And God helped him against the Philistines, and against the Arabians that dwelt in Gur-baal, and the Mehunim." Thus he avenged the Philistine invasion during the reign of Jehoram (2 Chronicles 21:16–17), and punished their allies. In 2 Chronicles 21 we read, "The LORD stirred up against Jehoram the spirit of the Philistines, and of the Arabians." This verse did not excuse them for their wrong-doing. They were the unconscious instruments used by God in the chastening of His people. Their motive was entirely of another kind, and after eighty years God meted out to them the punishment their attack on the land of Judah deserved. "God helped [Uzziah] against the Philistines, and against the Arabians." This is an important principle which must be remembered in any study of God's ways in government, with either men or nations (see Isaiah 10:5–19).

"And the Ammonites gave gifts to Uzziah: and his name was spread abroad even to the entering in of Egypt; for he strengthened himself exceedingly." He built towers in Jerusalem, and fortified them. He also "built towers in the desert" (the steppe-lands west of the Dead Sea), and cut out many cisterns; "for he had much cattle, both in the low country" (literally, "the Shepheleh," the low hills between the mountains and the Mediterranean), "and in the plains" (east of the Dead Sea). His wealth seems to have been chiefly in stock and agriculture. He had "husbandmen also, and vinedressers in the mountains, and in Carmel: for he loved husbandry." He was an earnest and successful agriculturist. He probably gave special attention to the tillage of the soil because of the prophecies of Hosea and Amos (his contemporaries) concerning the scarcity about to come (see Hosea 2:9; 4:3; 9:2; Amos 1:2; 4:6–9; 5:16–19).

He also gave attention to military matters, and thoroughly organized his army "that made war with mighty power, to help the king against the enemy." He saw too that his army was thoroughly equipped, as we read:

> And Uzziah prepared for them throughout all the host shields, and spears, and helmets, and [coats of mail], and bows, and slings to cast stones. And he made in Jerusalem engines invented by cunning men, to be upon the towers and upon the bulwarks, to shoot arrows and great stones withal. And his name spread far abroad; for he was marvellously helped, till he was strong (2 Chronicles 26:14–15).

Nevertheless, what is man! After all this well-doing, Uzziah's heart is lifted up with pride. Then came his act of sacrilege—the dark blot on the record of this otherwise blameless man's life. "But"—alas, those *buts* in so many life records of God's saints!—"when he was strong, his heart was lifted up to his destruction: for he transgressed against the Lord his God, and went into the temple of the Lord to burn incense upon the altar of incense"—explicitly forbidden by the law (see Exodus 30:7–8; Numbers 16:40; 18:7).

> And Azariah the priest went in after him, and with him fourscore priests of the LORD, that were valiant men: and they withstood Uzziah the king, and said unto him, It appertaineth not unto thee, Uzziah, to burn incense unto the LORD, but to the priests the sons of Aaron, that are consecrated to burn incense: go out of the sanctuary; for thou hast trespassed; neither shall it be for thine honour from the LORD God. Then Uzziah was wroth, and had a censer in his hand to burn incense: and while he was wroth with the priests, the leprosy even rose up in his forehead before the priests in the house of the LORD, from beside the incense altar. And Azariah the chief priest, and all the priests, looked upon him, and, behold, he was leprous in his forehead, and they thrust him out from thence; yea, himself hasted also to go out, because the LORD had smitten him. And Uzziah the king was a leper unto the day of his death, and dwelt in a several [separate] house, being a leper; for he was cut off from the house of the LORD (2 Chronicles 26:17–21).

It was a fearful stroke from God. Death was the actual penalty enjoined by the law for his crime (Numbers 18:7), and leprosy was really that—a living death, prolonged and intensified. "Let her not be as one dead, of whom the flesh is half consumed," was said of Miriam, who was smitten with a like judgment, and for a similar offense. God is holy, and must vindicate His word against every transgressor. He is no respecter of persons, and brings to light, sooner or later, every man's work and purposes of heart—including those of His best servants (see Numbers 12:10–12; 1 Timothy 5:24–25).

The driving motive in this audacious act of king Uzziah's is not made known. It has been suggested that he wished, like the Egyptian kings, to combine in himself both the office of king and high priest, so appropriating to himself the religious as well as the civil power. But whatever the immediate impelling motive, we know the primary cause of his profane deed. It was pride, the original sin, that hideous parent-sin of all succeeding sins, whether among angels or among men (1 Timothy 3:6; Ezekiel 28:2,17). "He was marvelously helped till he was strong. *But when he was strong,* his heart was lifted up to his destruction" (italics added). "Strength of Jehovah" was the meaning of Uzziah's name; and better would it have been for him had he realized that only in His strength is any really strong. "My strength," says He who is the Almighty, "is made perfect in weakness." "When I am weak, then am I strong," wrote one who knew his own utter powerlessness and his Lord's sufficient strength (2 Corinthians 12:9–10). "Be strong *in the* LORD," he cautioned his fellow weaklings. Uzziah prospered and because of his prosperity his foolish heart was lifted up with pride. In him was fulfilled his great ancestor's proverbs, "The prosperity of fools shall destroy them," and "Pride goeth before destruction, and an haughty spirit before a fall" (Proverbs 1:32; 16:18).

> Now the rest of the acts of Uzziah, first and last, did Isaiah the prophet, the son of Amoz, write. So Uzziah slept with his fathers, and they buried him with his fathers in the field of the burial which belonged to the kings; for they said, He is a leper: and Jotham his son reigned in his stead (2 Chronicles 26:22–23).

They would not lay his leprous body in their "Westminster Abbey," but buried him in a field (in earth, perhaps) adjoining the sepulchres of their kings. He died about the time of the founding of Rome. It was "in the year that king Uzziah died" that Isaiah began his full prophetic ministry (Isaiah 6:1). The moral condition of the nation during the close of Uzziah's reign is revealed in the first five chapters of Isaiah. He was also the historiographer of his reign. It is not known in just what year of Uzziah's reign he was smitten with leprosy. Nor is it certain just when the great earthquake occurred (Amos 1:1; Zechariah 14:5). From Amos 1:1, compared with other Scripture chronological references, it is quite certain that it occurred not later than seventeen years after Uzziah's accession to the throne, and not when he was smitten with leprosy, as Josephus mistakenly affirmed.

JOTHAM

Jehovah-perfect
(2 Kings 15:32–38; 2 Chronicles 27)

CONTEMPORARY PROPHETS: Isaiah, Micah, Hosea

Mercy and truth preserve the king: and his throne is upholden by mercy.

Proverbs 20:28

Jotham was twenty and five years old when he began to reign, and he reigned sixteen years in Jerusalem. His mother's name also was Jerushah, the daughter of Zadok" (2 Chronicles 27:1). Jotham was regent over the kingdom after the judgment of God fell upon his father: "And Jotham his son was over the king's house, judging the people of the land" (2 Chronicles 26:21). This would indicate that Uzziah was guilty of his irreverent trespass in the very last part of his long reign, as Jotham was only a young man of twenty-five at his father's death, and he could not have been judging the people of the land many years before this. His mother's name, *Jerushah* ("possessed"), daughter of *Zadok* ("just"), would seem to imply that she belonged to the Lord, and was considered just before Him. She, like every true mother, would influence her son considerably in the formation of his character. So we read, "And he did that which was right in the sight of the LORD, according to all that his father Uzziah did: *howbeit he entered not into the temple of the LORD*" (italics added). He avoided the folly of his headstrong father, and did not "rush in where angels fear to tread."

"And the people did yet corruptly" (27:2). The prophecies of Isaiah and Micah contain much detail of the manner of their wickedness, which was indeed great. It probably increased rapidly toward the close of Uzziah's reign, though from the beginning of his rule "the high places were not taken away: as yet the people did sacrifice and burnt incense on the high places" (2 Kings 14:4). True, the sacrifices and incense were offered to Jehovah, but Scripture said that Jerusalem was "the place where men ought to worship." This departure, though probably considered unimportant by many godly Israelites, paved the way for greater and more serious violations of the law. God's people are only safe as they adhere carefully and closely to the very letter of the word of God. The slightest digressions are often the prelude of wide and grave departures from obedience to God's will as revealed in His Word. The beginning of sin is, like strife, "as when one letteth out water" (Proverbs 17:14).

And "he built the high gate of the house of the LORD, and on the wall of Ophel he built much." The high gate led from the king's house to the temple (see 2 Chronicles 23:20), and

Jotham

Jotham's building it (rebuilding, or repairing) is very significant. He wished free access from his own house to that of the Lord. He would strengthen the link between the two houses—keep his line of communication open (to use a military figure) with the source of his supplies of strength and wisdom. This is one of the secrets of his prosperity and power.

"Moreover he built cities in the mountains of Judah, and in the forests he built castles and towers." He built where most men would have thought it unnecessary, or too much trouble—in the mountains and forests. He neglected no part of his kingdom, but sought to strengthen and fortify it everywhere. And as a result, he prospered.

> He fought also with the king of the Ammonites, and prevailed against them. And the children of Ammon gave him the same year a hundred talents of silver, and ten thousand measures of wheat, and ten thousand of barley. So much did the children of Ammon pay unto him, both the second year and the third. So Jotham became mighty, *because he prepared his ways before the* LORD *his God* (27:5–6, italics added).

That high gate between the palace and the temple was better than a Chinese wall around his kingdom. All real prosperity and power is found in communion with God.

"Now the rest of the acts of Jotham, and all his wars, and his ways, lo, they are written in the book of the kings of Israel and Judah." "*All* his wars" implies that during his sixteen years' reign he was actively engaged in conflict with enemies, subduing some, like the Ammonites, and repelling the invasions of others (Rezin king of Syria, and Pekah king of Israel). His "ways" too were written. God's saints are called to *walk,* as well as to war. "I have fought a good fight," said Paul the apostle, "I have finished my course," he also added. This last was his "ways." Ours, like king Jotham's, "are written in the book." May we then take heed to our ways! Jotham is the only one of all the Hebrew kings, from Saul down, against whom God has nothing to record. In this his character is in beautiful accord with his name, "Jehovah-perfect." "All have sinned," God says. But in his public life, Jotham, like Daniel, was perfect or blameless. Daniel's enemies said, "We shall not find any occasion against this Daniel, except we find it against him concerning the law of his God." Yet this same Daniel said, "I was . . . confessing my sin" (Daniel 6:5; 9:20). Man saw nothing to condemn: Daniel knew God's eye saw much. And, like the honest man that he was, he put it on record with his own hand that he had sins to be confessed to God.

"And Jotham slept with his fathers, and they buried him in the city of David: and Ahaz his son reigned in his stead." Did Micah have Jotham's death in mind when he wrote, "The good man is perished out of the earth" (Micah 7:2)? From what follows in that chapter, down to the seventh verse, it would appear so. The violence, fraud, bribery, treachery, and other forms of wickedness described in those verses, is just what prevailed after Jotham, under Ahaz' infamous rule. Jotham was indeed a godly man, and well might the righteous say on his death, "Help, Lord, for the godly man ceaseth" or, "is gone."

The record of Jotham's reign is brief, but full of brightness. His memory, like that of all the just, is blessed (Proverbs 10:7). He was the tenth of Judah's kings, and *God always claims His tithe;* in Jotham, the "Jehovah-perfect," it was found.

AHAZ

Possessor
(2 Kings 16; 2 Chronicles 28)

CONTEMPORARY PROPHETS: Isaiah, Micah, Hosea, Oded

It is an abomination to kings to commit wickedness: for the throne is established by righteousness.

Proverbs 16:12

Ahaz was as wicked as his father Jotham was righteous. It seems strange that the best of men frequently have the worst of sons.

Ahaz was twenty years old when he began to reign, and he reigned sixteen years in Jerusalem: but he did not that which was right in the sight of the LORD, like David his father: For he walked in the ways of the kings of Israel, and made also molten images for Baalim. Moreover he burnt incense in the valley of the son of Hinnom, and burnt his children in the fire, after the abominations of the heathen whom the LORD had cast out before the children of Israel. He sacrificed also and burnt incense in the high places [not removed in Jotham's day, 2 Kings 15:35], and on the hills, and under every green tree (2 Chronicles 28:1–4).

Ahaz' mother is not mentioned, and it is possible that his father was unfortunate in his choice of a wife. A king with the heavy responsibilities of government pressing constantly upon him can have little time to give to the training of his children: that important duty must fall largely on the mother. It was not every king of Judah that was blessed with such a mother as king Lemuel's (Proverbs 31).

But whoever or whatever Ahaz' mother may have been, he was himself responsible for his idolatrous deeds, and God punished him accordingly. "Wherefore the LORD his God delivered him into the hand of the king of Syria; and they smote him, and carried away a great multitude of them captives, and brought them to Damascus. And he was also delivered into the hand of the king of Israel, who smote him with a great slaughter" (2 Chronicles 28:5–6). These statements in no way clash with what is recorded in 2 Kings 16:5—that these confederate kings "could not overcome him." They could not get into the city, nor reach the king personally, though they entered the land. *They smote him,* means that they conquered his people and kingdom. Elath was also lost to Judah at this time (2 Kings 16:6).

We read in Isaiah 7 that it was the purpose of "the two tails of these smoking firebrands" to dethrone king Ahaz, and set up in his stead the son of *Tabeal* (probably a Syrian as it is not a Hebrew name). It was doubtless Satan's plot, if not man's, to destroy the Davidic dynasty, and for this reason, God did not deliver Jerusalem into their hands. But the slaughter and slavery of the people at large throughout the kingdom was something almost unparalleled (see 2 Chronicles 28:6). This is why Isaiah took with him his son *Shearjashub* ("the remnant shall return"), when he went out to meet king Ahaz. There should be a remnant left to return to the land; and the virgin would bear a son, so there should not fail a king on the throne of David. The dynasty could never be destroyed, for of Immanuel's kingdom there shall be no end (see Isaiah 7).

"Pekah the son of Remaliah slew in Judah a hundred and twenty thousand in one day, which were all valiant men"—the flower of Ahaz' army—"because they had forsaken the LORD God of their fathers." And though the king himself escaped, God's rod reached him through his son: "And Zichri, a mighty man of Ephraim, slew Maaseiah the king's son." He also slew the "governor of the house," and "Elkanah that was next to the king." How, or where, we know not. God can find the guilty where and when He will.

> And the children of Israel carried away captive of their brethren two hundred thousand, women, sons and daughters, and took away also much spoil from them, and brought the spoil to Samaria. But a prophet of the LORD was there, whose name was Oded: and he … said unto them, Behold, because the LORD God of your fathers was wroth with Judah, He hath delivered them into your hand, and ye have slain them in a rage that reacheth up unto heaven. And now ye purpose to keep under the children of Judah and Jerusalem for bondmen and bondwomen unto you: but are there not with you, even with you, sins against the LORD your God? [How many and

how great were Israel's sins!] Now hear me therefore, and deliver the captives again, which ye have taken captive of your brethren: for the fierce wrath of the LORD is upon you. [They were themselves, in a few short years, carried captive beyond Babylon.] Then certain of the heads of the children of Ephraim, Azariah the son of Johanan, Berechiah the son of Meshillemoth, and Jehizkiah the son of Shallum, and Amasa the son of Hadlai, stood up against them that came from the war, and said unto them, Ye shall not bring in the captives hither: for whereas we have offended against the LORD already, ye intend to add more to our sins and to our trespass: for our trespass is great, and there is fierce wrath against Israel (2 Chronicles 28:8–13).

Here is faithfulness and denunciation of sin where one might least expect it—in the city of Samaria, and from leaders, heads of the people. There were not ten righteous men in Sodom, and one might think that Samaria was not much better. But all there had not bowed the knee to Baal, and they spoke for truth and right with boldness in the very face of a returning, victorious army. Their words had the desired effect, for the wicked will sometimes give heed to the words of the righteous in a most wonderful way.

So the armed men left the captives and the spoil before the princes and all the congregation. And the men which were expressed by name rose up, and took the captives, and with the spoil clothed all that were naked among them, and arrayed them, and shod them, and gave them to eat and to drink, and anointed them, and carried all the feeble of them upon asses, and brought them to Jericho, the city of palm trees, to their brethren: then they returned to Samaria (14–15).

Ahaz

Their conduct was morally beautiful, especially when seen against the dark background of the evil times and kingdom in which they lived. And the righteous Lord who loveth righteousness has seen to it that these men of tender heart and upright conscience should be "expressed by name." The incident is like a little gleam of light shining out of the rapidly deepening darkness. The God of Israel has placed it on eternal record and published it abroad, that men might know that He never forgets a kindness done to His people, even when they suffer, under His authority, the just punishment of their sins.

"At that time did king Ahaz send unto the kings of Assyria to help him." The Edomites, surely emboldened by the success of Rezin and Pekah, invaded the land and "carried away captives." The Philistines also invaded "the low country, and the south of Judah," and settled themselves in the captured cities. "For the LORD brought Judah low because of Ahaz king of Israel; for he made Judah naked [lawless], and transgressed sore against the LORD."

The days were indeed dark: a cloud of gloom had settled over the once fair land and kingdom of David. Stroke succeeded stroke, and humiliation followed humiliation. But there was no national repentance, and the king (the responsible cause of it all) only hardened himself in rebellion and folly. The king of Assyria came, but instead of really helping him, "distressed him." He took the treasure Ahaz stripped for him from the house of the Lord, and from his own house, and the houses of the princes. It was just as the prophet Isaiah had forewarned him: "The LORD shall bring upon thee, and upon thy people, and upon thy father's house, days that have not come, from the day that Ephraim departed from Judah; even the king of Assyria" (Isaiah 7:17). He trusted in man, made flesh his arm, his heart departing from the Lord, and brought on himself and kingdom the consequent curse and barrenness (Jeremiah 17:5). "And in the time of his distress did he trespass yet more against the LORD." How different was his great ancestor David! "In my distress," he said, "I called upon the LORD, and cried unto my God" (Psalm 18:6). Even his wicked grandson Manasseh sought the Lord his God "when he was in affliction." But Ahaz seemed determined to fill up the measure of his sins. He was like the apostates of Christendom during the outpouring of "the vials of the wrath of God upon the earth." Though "they gnawed their tongues for pain," they still "blasphemed the God of heaven," and repented not of their deeds to give Him glory (Revelation 16). Each humiliating disaster, instead of turning Ahaz to God, drove him further into sin.

Oh, the blind delusion of demon-worship! "He sacrificed unto the gods of Damascus, *which smote him:* and he said, Because the gods of the kings of Syria help them, therefore will I sacrifice to them, that they may help me. But they were the ruin of him, and of all Israel" (2 Chronicles 28:23, italics added). He said, in effect, "Jehovah does not help me as the deities of the Syrian kings help them; so it is better for me to forsake Him and worship gods that will do me some good." So he "gathered together the vessels of the house of God, and cut in pieces the vessels of the house of God, and shut up the doors of the house of the LORD." His apostasy was now complete. "And he made him altars [for false gods] in every corner of Jerusalem. And in every several city of Judah he made high places to burn incense unto other gods, and provoked to anger the LORD God of his fathers." How far can they fall who, instead of being obedient to the word of God, are moved and governed by everything that offers some present, apparent success!

How shameful is his obsequious appeal to the king of Assyria: "I am thy servant and thy son: come up, and save me

Ahaz

out of the hand of the king of Syria" (2 Kings 16:7). And that monarch, greedy for the silver and gold sent him, went to Damascus and slew Rezin, its king.

> And king Ahaz went to Damascus to meet Tiglath-pileser king of Assyria [at his command perhaps, to do him honor personally] and saw an altar that was at Damascus: and king Ahaz sent to Urijah the priest the fashion of the altar, and the pattern of it, according to all the workmanship thereof. And Urijah the priest built an altar according to all that king Ahaz had sent from Damascus: so Urijah the priest made it against king Ahaz came from Damascus. And when the king was come from Damascus, the king saw the altar: and the king approached to the altar, and offered thereon. And he burnt his burnt offering and his meat offering, and poured his drink offering, and sprinkled the blood of his peace offerings, upon the altar (2 Kings 16:10–13).

The pattern of the altar caught his ritualistic eye, and he must needs imitate it—not unlike some today who will copy things they see in false religions. King Ahaz found in Urijah the high priest a willing tool to his idolatrous designs. Untrue to his name ("Sight of Jehovah"), he yielded unscrupulous obedience to his sovereign's orders, instead of rebuking him for his abominable act. Perhaps it was because of his degrading subserviency that his name is omitted from the sacred list in 1 Chronicles 6:4–15.

On this altar of new design Ahaz offered every kind of offering excepting that which he needed most for himself—the sin offering. The plain brazen altar ("which was before the house of the LORD") seems to have offended his appreciative eye, so it was relegated to a place of comparative obscurity on the north side of his own foreign altar. He arrogantly commanded the high priest as to what, and how, and when to offer on his altar. And the unworthy successor of Jehoiada and Zechariah slavishly obeyed to the letter. "Thus did Urijah the priest, according to all that king Ahaz commanded." He reversed the apostles' maxim, that we "ought to obey God rather than men." He was of another mind: his eye was on the honor that comes from man; theirs was on that which comes from God.

"And king Ahaz cut off the borders [or side panels] of the bases, and removed the laver from off them; and took down the sea from off the brazen oxen that were under it, and put it upon a pavement of stones." These sacrilegious innovations were probably introduced in order to obtain the precious metals of which these objects were made. "And the covert for the sabbath"—the covered way used on the sabbath by the royal worshipers—"that they had built in the house [of God], and the king's entry without, turned he from the house of the Lord for the king of Assyria" (2 Kings 16:18). It was the high gate that his father Jotham had so significantly rebuilt. Ahaz appears to have profaned it to the use of Tiglath-pileser when worshiping his false gods (at Ahaz' altar perhaps) on his visit to Jerusalem.

"And the brazen altar," he said, "shall be for me to inquire by," or "consider" (2 Kings 16:15). He either meant that he would use it for purposes of divination—linking Jehovah's great name with his base idolatries—or he would consider what should ultimately be done with it. And we Christians have an altar, even Christ, our Creator-Redeemer, whom profane Unitarian critics and others dare to debase and degrade before their deceived disciples, removing Him from His place of absolute preeminence (like Ahaz with God's altar), putting Him beside others, like Zoroaster and Confucius. And already they consider what they shall finally do with

Him—relegate Him to a place even of inferiority to some of their heathen Asiatic reformers! And what shall the end be? We know: "Another shall come in his own name, [and] him [they] will receive" (John 5:43). The man of sin—the son of perdition—is to arise; and "because they received not the love of the truth, that they might be saved...God shall send them strong delusion, that they should believe a lie" (2 Thessalonians 2:10–11).

"Now the rest of his acts and of all his ways, first and last, behold, they are written in the book of the kings of Judah and Israel" (2 Chroniclses 28:26). God too has *ways* and *acts*. "He made known his ways unto Moses, his acts unto the children of Israel" (Psalm 103:7). His ways were the manifestations of His nature; His acts more the displays of His power. And what manifestations of the wickedness of Ahaz' heart did his life of thirty-six years bring out! It is little wonder that the inspiring Spirit led the chronicler to call him king of *Israel* (2 Chronicles 28:19)—he was so like the nineteen idolatrous rulers of the northern kingdom. Even his people who shared in his wickedness are called *Israel,* instead of Judah (2 Chronicles 28:23). But there must have been some sense of righteousness (or shame) left in them; for we read, "They buried him in the city, even in Jerusalem: but they brought him not into the sepulchres of the kings of Israel." Corrupt as they themselves were, they felt that their late king had so exceeded in wickedness that it was not fitting to lay his body among those of his royal ancestors.

The Philistines, who had good cause to fear the kings of Judah, had a special prophecy written for them by Isaiah at this time, bidding them not to rejoice at king Ahaz' death (see Isaiah 14:28–32). He appears to have been little influenced by the faithful ministry of the evangelist-prophet. Ahaz was apparently a man of aesthetic tastes (as even the ungodliest of men may be), from his admiration of the Damascus altar. He was also interested in the sciences, it would seem, from his introduction into Jerusalem of the Chaldean sundial (2 Kings 20:11). Nor was he of a persecuting spirit apparently, for he did not, like his grandson Manasseh, shed innocent blood nor put to death the prophets. He was possessed (*Ahaz* means "possessor") of much that men admire and magnify today, but without godliness all this is of absolutely no worth. Apparently impenitent to the last, he died as he had lived: "and Hezekiah his son reigned in his stead."

HEZEKIAH

Strength of Jehovah
(2 Kings 18–21; 2 Chronicles 29–32; Isaiah 38–39)

CONTEMPORARY PROPHETS: Isaiah, Micah, Nahum, Hosea

The king by judgment establisheth the land: but he that receiveth gifts overthroweth it.

Proverbs 29:4

"Hezekiah began to reign when he was five and twenty years old, and he reigned nine and twenty years in Jerusalem." We are confronted here with what has been considered one of the greatest chronological difficulties of the Bible. In few words, it is this: Scripture says that Ahaz, Hezekiah's father, began his reign when he was twenty years of age, and he reigned sixteen years in Jerusalem. And Hezekiah, it says, was twenty-five years old when he ascended the throne. This seems to teach that Ahaz was but eleven years old when Hezekiah his son was born, which is altogether unlikely, if not impossible. Josephus did not touch on the difficulty; he possibly felt there was none. Modern commentators have suggested various solutions of the problem, none of which is satisfactory. Fausset said "twenty" in 2 Kings 16:2 is "a transcriber's error" for *twenty-five,* citing the Septuagint, Syriac, and Arabic manuscripts of 2 Chronicles 28:1. But in reply to this, someone pertinently wrote: "We may observe, that it is never advisable to find any fault with the text except where there is no other tolerable solution, which is not the case here." The Septuagint and other versions reading "twenty-five" for *twenty* in 2 Chronicles 28:1 prove nothing, except that the transcribers may have tampered with the original text in order to get rid of a seemingly inexplicable difficulty.

Two legitimate explanations offer themselves. First, it is quite possible a break of some years may have occurred in king Ahaz' reign, either when he went to Damascus to meet Tiglath-pileser (2 Kings 16:10) or, which seems more likely, when the king of Assyria came to Jerusalem and "distressed him" (2 Chronicles 28:20–21; 2 Kings 16:18). It would not be at all unlike these Assyrian kings for Tiglath-pileser to temporarily depose the king of Judah during his sojourn in those parts. Second, Scripture does not say that Hezekiah began to reign *immediately* after the death of his father. True, the usual form of words is used—"Ahaz slept with his fathers ... and Hezekiah his son reigned in his stead" (2 Chronicles 28:27). But similar words are used in 2 Kings 15:30: "And Hoshea the son of Elah made a conspiracy against Pekah the son of Remaliah, and smote him, and slew him, and reigned in his stead." In point of fact, he did not actually begin to reign until at least nine years later, as Scripture chronologists are generally agreed (compare 2 Kings 16:1 and 17:1). So Scripture permits us to believe that a number of years may have elapsed between the death of Ahaz (owing to the unsettled state of his kingdom) and the accession of Hezekiah. This would entirely do away with any difficulty as to Ahaz' immature age at the birth of his firstborn.

In support of the first explanation it must be remembered that it is nothing unusual in Scripture to take no note of interruptions or breaks in chronology. Compare 1 Kings 6:1 and Acts 13:18–22; the first, 480 years; the second, 573—a difference of ninety-three years. This difference is just the number of years of Israel's five servitudes of 8, 18, 20, 7, and 40 years, under Mesopotamia, Moab, Canaan, Midian, and Philistia, respectively (see Judges 3:8; 3:14; 4:3; 6:1; 13:1). The Ammonite oppression must be omitted, not being truly in the land but "on the other side Jordan" (see Judges 10:8), just as several generations are frequently omitted in the genealogies. If it is suggested that either of these solutions would interfere with the harmony of the table of dates in this volume, it is replied that there is absolutely no positive proof that the break between the reigns of Pekah and Hoshea was of nine years' duration. The calculation is based wholly on the figures used in reference to Ahaz and Hezekiah. As to any interference with late Old Testament chronology as a whole, it needs only to be said that chronologists are by no means agreed here, as in other portions of the Old Testament. Nor are the Hebrew, Septuagint, and Samaritan texts in harmony as to dates. God seems purposely to have left the matter of dates somewhat undecided; nor is it for us to know the times or the seasons, which the Father hath put in His own power.

But we proceed with Hezekiah: "His mother's name was Abija, the daughter of Zechariah." Her father was perhaps one of the two faithful witnesses of Isaiah 8:2. Or, she may have been a descendant of the Zechariah who guided Uzziah during the earlier portion of his reign; or even of the martyr Zechariah, who was slain by order of king Joash. Anyway, she must have been a true mother in Israel to have raised so godly a son, with such a wicked father's example before him. Mothers, what a responsibility is yours, and what a privilege as well, to have God, as it were, say to you, "Take this child, and nurse it for Me, and I will give thee thy wages." Abija surely had her wages when she saw her son renew and reform the desolated kingdom of his father David. Frequently, in truth, the hand that rocks the cradle rules the empire, whether it be for blessing or for cursing.

"And he did that which was right in the sight of the LORD, according to all that David his father did." If, as has been remarked, Ahaz was an extraordinarily bad man to have come of so good a father, so here the reverse is true: Hezekiah was a remarkably good man, with so notably wicked a father. How true the wise Preacher's reflection as to one's successors, whether it be in a kingdom or a smaller household, "Who knoweth whether he shall be a wise man or a fool?" (Ecclesiastes 2:19).

Hezekiah began to manifest immediately what manner of king he would be.

> He in the first year of his reign, in the first month, opened the doors of the house of the LORD [which Ahaz his father had shut up], and repaired them. And he brought in the priests and the Levites, and gathered them together into the east street, And said unto them, Hear me, ye Levites; sanctify now yourselves, and sanctify the house of the LORD God of your fathers, and carry forth the filthiness out of the holy place (2 Chronicles 29:3–5).

Hezekiah

He began at the only right place—the sanctuary; and at the right time—immediately—without delay, in the *first* day of the *first* month of the *first* year of his reign (2 Chronicles 29:17). Whatever reforms were needed elsewhere in the kingdom, this must have precedence over them all. Other things could not be really right if this were wrong. Revival, with God, is like His judgment—it must begin at His house (see Ezekiel 9:6; 1 Peter 4:17). "Let them make me a sanctuary; that I may dwell among them," was Jehovah's gracious command to them at the very beginning of their existence as a nation (Exodus 25:8). Solomon said in his prayer, "That thine eyes may be open toward this house night and day, even toward the place of which thou hast said, my name shall be there" (1 Kings 8:29). The temple was to the kingdom as the heart to the body—when it ceased to pulsate with activity and life, the body politic, or nation, could not but languish, stagnate, and die. If God had chosen them as His own peculiar nation out of all the rest, He must have the central place among them. His authority and claims must be recognized if they wished to be prospered by Him. So it is in this day of church dispensation.

"My sons," Hezekiah called the priests and Levites, in true fatherly love to them, as every king should have toward his people (2 Chronicles 29:11). *The everlasting Father* is one of the titles of our Lord Christ who, as God's model King, shall reign over the happy inhabitants of the millennial earth in the glorious day now not far off (see Isaiah 9:6).

"Then the Levites arose...and they gathered their brethren, and sanctified themselves, and came, according to the commandment of the king, by the words of the LORD, to cleanse the house of the LORD." On the eighth day the work was finished, the sabbath, probably; and on the sixteenth day "they made an end" (2 Chronicles 29:12–17). They began at the inner sanctuary, and ended at the porch. God always works from within—not like man, from the outside. God looks on the heart, and is not, like man, satisfied with a fair external appearance.

"Moreover all the vessels, which king Ahaz in his reign did cast away in his transgressions," they resanctified, and set them before the altar of burnt offering, which they had also cleansed, with the shewbread table. "Then Hezekiah the king rose up early, and gathered the rulers of the city, and went up to the house of the LORD." There they offered "a sin offering for the kingdom, and for the sanctuary, and for Judah." Then an atonement was made for all Israel: "for the king commanded that the burnt offering and the sin offering should be made for *all Israel*" (24). His fatherly heart went out toward all the tribes. He loved and thought of them all, even though the bulk of them were divided from him, and subjects of the murderous conspirator Hoshea. He set Levites in the temple with cymbals, psalteries, and harps, and the priests stood with the trumpets. "And when the burnt offering began, the song of the LORD began also with the trumpets, and with the instruments ordained by David king of Israel" (27). It was a wonderful day for Jerusalem; the number of offerings brought by the people was so large that the priests could not skin them all, and had to be assisted by the Levites. "So," we read, "the service of the house of God was set in order. And Hezekiah rejoiced, and all the people, that God had prepared the people: for the thing was done suddenly" (36).

And now comes what may be considered the crowning act of this excellent king's life.

> And Hezekiah sent to all Israel and Judah, and wrote letters also to Ephraim and Manasseh, that they should come to the house of the LORD at Jerusalem, to keep the passover unto the

LORD God of Israel. For the king had taken counsel, and his princes, and all the congregation in Jerusalem, to keep the passover in the second month. For they could not keep it at that time, because the priests had not sanctified themselves sufficiently, neither had the people gathered themselves together to Jerusalem. And the thing pleased the king and all the congregation (2 Chronicles 30:1–4).

There was beautiful harmony between king and people. All was done willingly by everyone. It was not as with Abijah, who "*commanded* Judah to seek the LORD God of their fathers" (2 Chronicles 14:4). Instead of commanding, Hezekiah consulted with the people here. "So *they*," not the king only, "established a decree to make proclamation throughout all Israel, from Beer-sheba even to Dan, that they should come to keep the passover unto the LORD God of Israel at Jerusalem: for they had not done it for a long time in such sort as it was written" (5). This may mean that before this the passover had been entirely neglected, or that it had been a long time since it was kept in the second month "as it was written" in Numbers 9:10–11.

If the first suggested meaning is the right one, what a condition the nation must have been in to have discontinued for a long time the primary and most significant of all their yearly feasts.

This revival in the very beginning of Hezekiah's reign is all the more remarkable in that it immediately succeeded what was probably the darkest period the kingdom of Judah had ever known. "Man's extremity is God's opportunity," certainly; and it is very frequently, if not always, "darkest just before dawn."

Messengers carried these circular letters of invitation throughout all Judah and Israel, saying:

Ye children of Israel, turn again unto the LORD God of Abraham, Isaac, and Israel, and he will return to the remnant of you, that are escaped out of the hand of the kings of Assyria.... For if ye turn again unto the LORD, your brethren and your children shall find compassion before them that led them captive, so that they shall come again into this land: for the LORD your God is gracious and merciful, and will not turn away his face from you, if ye return unto him (2 Chronicles 30:6–9).

It was a beautiful message, holding out comfort and hope to the sorrowing remnant of Israel, who had seen so many of their loved ones led away in bondage to the land of the Assyrian.

So the message was carried throughout the country. Some, as we see, were glad of the exhortation (those who had suffered most from the Assyrian, probably). Ephraim, the "cake not turned," and others impiously and impudently mocked, and made light of the messengers and their message. It is not the only occasion on which God's message received this scornful treatment. Seven hundred years later, and seven hundred miles away, at Mars Hill in Athens, Paul delivered a more solemn message from his God but with like result: "some mocked," while certain "clave unto him and believed" (Acts 17). And it is the same today. Have you believed God's gospel message, and, like some of Asher and Manasseh and of Zebulun, humbled yourself, and come to Jesus?

"And there assembled at Jerusalem much people to keep the feast of unleavened bread in the second month, a very great congregation" (2 Chronicles 30:13). They removed the unlawful altars found in the city "and cast them into the brook Kidron." They killed and ate the passover according to the law, as nearly as could be done under the circumstances. "For a multitude of the people, even many of Ephraim and

Hezekiah

Manasseh, Issachar, and Zebulun, had not cleansed themselves, yet did they eat the passover otherwise than it was written. But Hezekiah prayed for them, saying, The good Lord pardon every one that prepareth his heart to seek God, the LORD God of his fathers, though he be not cleansed according to the purification of the sanctuary" (18–19). He made intercession for the people in the spirit of the future King who shall be "a priest upon his throne" (Zechariah 6:13). "And the LORD hearkened to Hezekiah, and healed the people."

The feast was kept with great gladness, with praise to God day by day on instruments of praise. "And Hezekiah spake comfortably unto all the Levites that taught the good knowledge of the LORD." As in all true revivals, the Scriptures had their place. And how much the poor recovered people needed the instruction given them by these Levites. Everyone rejoiced (as well they might) and it was unanimously agreed to celebrate seven more days. "So there was great joy in Jerusalem: for since the time of Solomon the son of David king of Jerusalem there was not the like in Jerusalem. Then the priests the Levites arose and blessed the people [see Numbers 6:23–26]: and their voice was heard, and their prayer came up to his holy dwelling place, even unto heaven" (2 Chronicles 30:26–27).

And then appears the practical result of this wonderful fourteen-day general meeting.

> Now when all this was finished, all Israel that were present went out to the cities of Judah, and brake the images in pieces, and cut down the groves, and threw down the high places and the altars out of all Judah and Benjamin, in Ephraim also and Manasseh, until they had utterly destroyed them all. Then all the children of Israel returned every man to his possession, into their own cities (31:1).

Hezekiah then restored to order the priestly and Levitical services of the temple, "as it is written in the law of the LORD. Moreover he commanded the people that dwelt in Jerusalem to give the portion of the priests and the Levites, that they might be encouraged in the law of the LORD" (31:3–4). There was an immediate and generous response to this thoughtful call of the king. "The children of Israel brought in abundance the firstfruits of corn, wine, and oil, and honey, and of all the increase of the field; and the tithe of all things brought they in abundantly." This awakening to their responsibilities towards those who ministered in holy things was not confined to the inhabitants of Jerusalem; it extended itself to all the kingdom. "And concerning the children of Israel and Judah, that dwelt in the cities of Judah, they also brought in the tithe of oxen and sheep, and the tithe of holy things" (31:5).

The offering continued from the third to the seventh month —all through their harvest and vintage—and was stored in heaps. "And when Hezekiah and the princes came and saw the heaps, they blessed the LORD and his people Israel." And it was appropriate that they should do so, for here in these material fruits of the land they witnessed the fruit of God's Spirit in His people. When the king questioned the priests and Levites concerning the accumulation, the chief priest "answered him and said, Since the people began to bring in the offerings into the house of the LORD, we have had enough to eat"—alas, that it should ever have been otherwise with them —"and have left plenty: for the LORD hath blessed his people; and that which is left is this great store." Chambers were prepared in the temple, by Hezekiah's command, to house this superabundant store. And they "brought in the offerings and the tithes and the dedicated things faithfully." Arrangements were made and officers appointed for the proper distribution of the stockpile. Everything was done in systematic order, according to the king's commandment.

> And thus did Hezekiah throughout all Judah, and wrought that which was good and right and truth before the LORD his God. And in every work that he began in the service of the house of God, and in the law, and in the commandments, to seek his God, he did it with all his heart [the only way to do anything] and prospered (31:20–21).

He was like the happy man of Psalm 1, of whom it is said, "Whatsoever he doeth shall prosper." This was John's highest wish for the beloved and hospitable Gaius (3 John 2). And it is written of the best Beloved of all, "The pleasure of the LORD shall prosper in his hand" (Isaiah 53:10).

Having set in order the spiritual matters of the kingdom, Hezekiah turned to the more material things in his dominion. "He smote the Philistines, even unto Gaza, and the borders thereof, from the tower of the watchman to the fenced city" (2 Kings 18:8). Then was fulfilled that which was spoken by the prophet Isaiah, in the year that king Ahaz died: "Rejoice not thou, whole Palestina, because the rod of him that smote thee [Uzziah] is broken [in Ahaz' death]: for out of the serpent's root [as they regarded him] shall come forth a cockatrice [Hezekiah], and his fruit shall be a fiery flying serpent" (Isaiah 14:29).

"And he rebelled against the king of Assyria, and served him not" (2 Kings 18:7). It would seem that this attempt to throw off the yoke of Assyria was premature, or perhaps the good king went beyond his faith; for when Sennacherib invaded his kingdom, we are pained to read that he took all the fortified cities. And Hezekiah weakened and sent to him at Lachish his submission, saying, "I have offended; return from me: that which thou puttest on me will I bear" (14). This was humiliating, though he does not grovel like his worthless father saying,

"I am thy son." His desire was right, but he may, in his zeal for the prosperity and glory of his kingdom, have anticipated God's time. Because of their former sins, Israel had become subject to the Assyrian, whom God had called the rod of His anger. Even though the nation was restored to righteousness under Hezekiah, God in His wise yet gracious government allowed the people to suffer awhile for their past, that they might fully realize by bitter and humiliating experience what a serious thing it is to turn from the living God to idols. So, poor Hezekiah (how we feel for the esteemed man!) pays the heavy fine imposed on him—"three hundred talents of silver and thirty talents of gold." To obtain this enormous amount, he had to almost strip bare the recently restored house of God and his palace of their treasures and utensils of silver and gold. He even had to remove the gold that his own loving hands had but recently laid on the temple doors and its pillars. How it must have hurt his great and righteous heart to strip God's dwelling place of its wealth of glory! And all because of his own hasty action, he might think.

This was in the fourteenth year of his reign (2 Kings 18:13). Fausset said *fourteenth* is a copyist's error for *twenty-seventh*. But we hear too much about these "copyist's errors." *Fourteenth* agrees with Isaiah 36:1 and harmonizes with Isaiah 38:5. It may be for lack of faith that men try hard to make Scripture square with secular history, or what purports to be history. Just because a date in the Bible does not come out even with Babylonian or Assyrian chronology, or disagrees with some untrustworthy heathen inscription, commentators cry, "transcriber's error"; as if imperfectly deciphered monuments and clay tablets must correct the word of God! *Fourteen* agrees with other portions and dates contained in Scripture, so it is perfectly satisfactory, whatever Assyriologists or commentators influenced by them may say.

Hezekiah

Sennacherib, for some reason or other, did not leave Hezekiah, as he had hoped. Perhaps it was impossible for Hezekiah to obtain the sum demanded by the king of Assyria; or that villainous plunderer, after receiving the required amount, may have changed his mind (if he ever really meant to let the king of Jerusalem buy him off), and determined to take possession of Hezekiah's capital before he left the country. His intention became known to Hezekiah, "and he took counsel with his princes and mighty men." They agreed to resist Sennacherib's capture of the city, and extensive preparations were made for the threatened siege. When all had been done that man could do, Hezekiah gathered the people "together to him in the street of the gate of the city," and addressed them with words of faith and courage: "Be strong and courageous," he said, "be not afraid nor dismayed for the king of Assyria, nor for all the multitude that is with him: for there be more with us than with him. With him is an arm of flesh; but with us is the LORD our God to help us, and to fight our battles" (2 Chronicles 32:7–8). These were fine words and very different from his saying a short time before to Sennacherib, "I have offended." His faith, though faint, had not altogether failed. Here it rises to its full height, and like the restored Simon Peter, he is able by his words and example to strengthen his brethren. "And the people rested themselves upon the words of Hezekiah king of Judah."

"After this did Sennacherib king of Assyria send his servants to Jerusalem . . . unto Hezekiah king of Judah, and unto all Judah that were at Jerusalem" (2 Chronicles 32:9). Then follows a harangue that for insolence and craftiness has never been exceeded. Rab-shakeh (a title, not a name), Sennacherib's commander-in-chief, was the speaker. Evidently he was an accomplished diplomat and delivered his artful speech in the Jews' language. He, with his fellow-officers, "stood by the conduit of the upper pool, which is in the highway of the fuller's field"—on an elevation, probably. Hezekiah's cabinet ministers interrupted him in his discourse, saying, "Speak, I pray thee, to thy servants in the Syrian language; for we understand it: and talk not with us in the Jews' language in the ears of the people that are on the wall" (2 Kings 18:26). They little knew the wily Rab-shakeh who, gaining an advantage by their fear, answered: "Hath my master sent me to thy master, and to thee, to speak these words? hath he not sent me to the men which sit on the wall?... Then Rab-shakeh stood and cried with a loud voice in the Jews' language, and spake, saying." He does his best to frighten the populace, which had been "shut up like a bird in a cage," as Sennacherib's own inscription states. He hoped to incite sedition in the city, in order to get possession without laying siege to it. But he labored in vain; "the people held their peace, and answered him not a word: for the king's commandment was, saying, Answer him not" (36).

His speech produced distress, however, and the king's officers came to Hezekiah "with their clothes rent, and told him the words of Rab-shakeh." And Hezekiah "rent his clothes, and covered himself with sackcloth, and went into the house of the LORD" (2 Kings 19:1). He turned to the true source of comfort in the dark hour; and also sent to Isaiah the prophet, saying,

> Thus saith Hezekiah, This day is a day of trouble, and of rebuke, and blasphemy [for Sennacherib's servants had spoken against the Lord God, against the God of Jerusalem]: for the children are come to the birth, and there is not strength to bring forth. It may be the LORD thy God will hear all the words of Rab-shakeh, whom the king of Assyria his master hath sent to reproach the living God; and will reprove the words which

the LORD thy God hath heard: wherefore lift up thy prayer for the remnant that are left (3–4).

The prophet's reply is brief and decisive: "And Isaiah said unto them, Thus shall ye say to your master, Thus saith the LORD, Be not afraid of the words which thou hast heard, with which the servants of the king of Assyria have blasphemed me. Behold, I will send a blast upon him, and he shall hear a rumor, and shall return to his own land; and I will cause him to fall by the sword in his own land" (6–7).

Sennacherib, anxious to leave the country, yet unwilling to let such a stronghold as Jerusalem remain untaken, dispatched a letter to the king, hoping against hope to frighten him into capitulation. "And Hezekiah received the letter of the hand of the messengers, and read it: and Hezekiah went up into the house of the LORD, and spread it before the LORD." How beautiful his childlike trust in the God of Israel! And there in the temple he prayed as only a saint in his hour of distress can pray (read 2 Kings 19:15–19). God answered him through a message from Isaiah, in which full deliverance is assured him.

> Therefore [it concludes] thus saith the LORD concerning the king of Assyria, He shall not come into this city, nor shoot an arrow there, nor come before it with shield, nor cast a bank against it. By the way that he came, by the same shall he return, and shall not come into this city, saith the LORD. For I will defend this city, to save it, for mine own sake, and for my servant David's sake. And it came to pass that night, that the angel of the LORD went out, and smote in the camp of the Assyrians an hundred fourscore and five thousand: and when they [or men] arose early in the morning, behold, they were all dead corpses. So Sennacherib king of Assyria departed, and

went and returned, and dwelt at Nineveh. And it came to pass, as he was worshipping in the house of Nisroch his god, that Adrammelech and Sharezer his sons smote him with the sword: and they escaped into the land of Armenia (32–37).

"So let all thine enemies perish, O LORD; but let them that love him be as the sun when he goeth forth in his might" (Judges 5:31). "Thus the LORD saved Hezekiah and the inhabitants of Jerusalem from the hand of Sennacherib the king of Assyria, and from the hand of all other, and guided [literally, protected] them on every side" (2 Chronicles 32:22).

"In those days was Hezekiah sick unto death." "Those days" must refer to the time of the Assyrian invasion, or immediately after Sennacherib came up, in the fourteenth year of Hezekiah's reign, for we read that the prophet said fifteen years would be added to his life. As he reigned twenty-nine years, there is no difficulty whatever in fixing the exact time of his sickness. Men make difficulties for themselves (where there really are none) by giving heed to uncertain monumental records, instead of abiding by the simple and sure statements of Holy Scripture.

"And the prophet Isaiah the son of Amoz came to him, and said unto him, Thus saith the LORD, Set thy house in order; for thou shalt die, and not live" (2 Kings 20:1). At the time of Sennacherib's attack on the city Isaiah had not gone personally to him, but sent word by a messenger. Some have thought from this and from certain passages in his prophecy that there was a coolness, or even estrangement, between the prophet and the king over his rebellion against Assyria. More likely it was the prophet's age (he must have been near eighty) that prevented him from going to the king. We can understand however that when Hezekiah lay at the point of death, the prophet would make a special effort to see him face to face.

Hezekiah

He was sent with heavy tidings to the childless king; and little wonder it was that the announcement of his death distressed him.

True to his habit and faith in God, Hezekiah turned to Him in distress; and almost before he called, God answered. The prophet had not yet reached the middle court when God said to him,

> Turn again, and tell Hezekiah the captain of my people, Thus saith the LORD, the God of David thy father, I have heard thy prayer, I have seen thy tears: behold, I will heal thee: on the third day thou shalt go up unto the house of the LORD. And I will add unto thy days fifteen years; and I will deliver thee and this city out of the hand of the king of Assyria; and I will defend this city for mine own sake, and for my servant David's sake (5–6).

His **full recovery was on the** *third day.* It is the day of resurrection (see Hosea 6:2), and on that day Judah received her king as if from the dead.

His cure was **in answer to prayer,** though means were used—a lump of figs. It is often more humble, and more according to God, to use means than not to use them. If the incident is typical, and the king's recovery on the third day (answering to the passage in Hosea) foreshadows Israel's national restoration, or resurrection, as in Daniel 12:2, we would naturally connect the lump of figs with Matthew 21:19–21 and 24:32. In those verses the fig tree is a figure of Israel, now under death and the curse of God, but yet to revive and bear fruit. This is not insisted upon, but only suggested. But as "God's commandment is exceeding broad," so is His blessed Word very full, and it is not of any private (or separate) interpretation.

KINGS OF JUDAH

Hezekiah quite properly asked for a sign to assure himself of his recovery. His hypocritical father, in mock modesty, refused to ask for a sign. He used a pious phrase in his refusal, saying, "I will not tempt the LORD." But he was not asked to "tempt God." God Himself had told him to ask for a sign. Unbelief and self-will were at the bottom of his blank refusal, though covered under this pious phrase. And he was not the last of religious unbelievers to use the same expression, and for a like purpose (see Isaiah 7).

God gave the anxious king a sign; and a wonderful sign it was. The shadow turned back on the dial of Ahaz ten degrees, in answer to the prophet's prayer. It was a miracle whatever way we take it. God could have reversed the revolution of the earth, had He seen fit to do so, for he is a poor clock maker who cannot turn the hands of his own workmanship backward. Or He could have caused the phenomenon by the ordinary law of refraction, or even by volcanic pressure from beneath He could have altered the inclination of the dial's column for the time being. In any case it was a miracle, whatever the rationalist or skeptical astronomer may say to the contrary.

The news of this miracle reached Chaldea, and a deputation was sent from Babylon "to inquire of the wonder that was done in the land." And it was in the business of these ambassadors that the recovered king was ensnared with pride. The letter and the present from the king of Babylon were too much for his latent vanity—native to us all. What Sennacherib's letter and deputation of offensive diplomats could not effect (for they drove him to his knees), the letter and friendly commission from Merodach-baladan accomplished—to his ruin almost, and that of his kingdom. How like the Christian and this world! Its *frown* is comparatively powerless; it is its subtle *favor* that we have most to fear.

Hezekiah rendered not again according to the benefit done unto him; for his heart was lifted up: therefore there was wrath upon him, and upon Judah and Jerusalem. Notwithstanding Hezekiah humbled himself for the pride of his heart, both he and the inhabitants of Jerusalem, so that the wrath of the LORD came not upon them in the days of Hezekiah (2 Chronicles 32:25–26).

It was not *spiritual* pride, as with his great-grandfather Uzziah, but *worldly* pride—the pride of life, we might say. It was *his* precious things, *his* armor, *his* treasures, *his* house, *his* dominion, that he showed the ambassadors from Babylon. When the prophet came to reprove him, he significantly asked, "What have they seen in *thine* house?" "All the things that is in *mine* house have they seen," Hezekiah answered; "there is nothing among *my* treasures that I have not showed them." Why did he not show these learned heathen *God's* house? There he could have explained to them the meaning of the brazen altar, and the sacrifices offered thereon. Who can tell what the result might have been in the souls of these idolaters? They were brought to Hezekiah's very doors by one of God's wonders in creation; why did he not embrace the opportunity of showing them of His higher wonders of redemption? But no; they were shown what displayed the glory of the poor pride-filled king. The "benefit done to him" was apparently forgotten. He did not ask, like his great father David, "What shall I render unto the LORD for all his benefits toward me?" and who also said, "*Forget not* all [God's] benefits." And we Christians, in a very much higher sense, have been made "partakers of the benefit." May we, in return, render unto God the glory due His name.

In 2 Chronicles 32:31 we read that "God left him, to try him, that he might know what was in his heart" (see Deuteronomy 8:2). Hezekiah learned, to his shame and sorrow, that there was a vast amount of *ego* there. It was well to know it, that it might be judged and put away before he would be betrayed by it into deeper and more serious sin. But when he heard the judgment pronounced by the prophet on his posterity, he meekly submitted, and said, "Good is the word of the LORD which thou hast spoken. He said moreover, For there shall be peace and truth in my days" (Isaiah 39:8). Someone aptly commented on Hezekiah's answer to Isaiah that it was "not the language of mere selfishness, but of one feeling that the national corruption must at last lead to the threatened judgment; and thanking God for the stroke being deferred yet for a time."

"And Hezekiah had exceeding much riches and honour." "God had given him substance very much." "And Hezekiah prospered in all his works." His scribes copied out a selection of Solomon's proverbs (Proverbs 25:1). Isaiah and other chroniclers recorded "the rest of his acts and goodness."

"And Hezekiah slept with his fathers, and they buried him in the chiefest of the sepulchres of the sons of David: and all Judah and the inhabitants of Jerusalem did him honour at his death. And Manasseh his son reigned in his stead" (2 Chronicles 32:33).

Of all the kings of Judah since the days of Solomon, Hezekiah is the shining light. It was left to him to break in pieces the brazen serpent made by Moses in the wilderness. It had become a snare to the nation; for up to Hezekiah's day they had burned incense to it. His reforming predecessors had lacked either the discernment to see the element of idolatry in the superstitious reverence shown it, or more probably they lacked the holy courage to destroy it in the face of popular opposition. It had been used by God in the wilderness as a type of Christ made sin for our salvation, but the nation had degraded it (and themselves) by regarding it with a semi-idolatrous spirit. Hezekiah, to his honor be it said, did not hesitate to remove this occasion of offense, calling it what it really was—"a [mere] piece of brass" (Nehushtan; 2 Kings 18:4).

"And the rest of the acts of Hezekiah, and all his might, and how he made a pool, and a conduit, and brought water into the city, are they not written in the book of the chronicles of the kings of Judah?" (2 Kings 20:20).

MANASSEH

Forgetting
(2 Kings 21:1–18; 2 Chronicles 33:1–20)

CONTEMPORARY PROPHET: Joel

The king sent and loosed him; even the ruler of the people, and let him go free.

Psalm 105:20

Manasseh was twelve years old when he began to reign, and he reigned fifty and five years in Jerusalem: but did that which was evil in the sight of the LORD, like unto the abominations of the heathen, whom the LORD had cast out before the children of Israel." His mother's name was *Hephzibah* ("my delight is in her," see Isaiah 62:4). She may have been a pious woman, and so her name may have been appropriate to her character. But if so, she had very little influence over her son—unlike the *Eunice* ("victorious") of a later day, and many more besides.

Extremes meet here, for Manasseh, one of the worst and most cruel of kings that ever reigned, succeeded Hezekiah, of whom it was said, "After him was none like him among all the kings of Judah, nor any that were before him" (2 Kings 18:5). Had this good king been able to foresee the wickedness of his unworthy son, he would doubtless have had no desire to recover from his sickness. Better by far to die childless than beget a son such as Manasseh proved to be. We must not presume to judge God's honored servant, but it does appear as if Hezekiah would have done better to have meekly submitted to God's will in his sickness. He could surely have left the matter of his successor with God, as he knew the covenant God had made with David. He may thus have spared the nation that he loved the tears and blood (to say nothing of God's honor in the matter) that his desired descendant brought to them. Nothing honorable is recorded to have been done by Hezekiah after his recovery from his sickness. True, his healing was in answer to prayer, and a wonderful miracle was done in pledge of it. But so it was with Israel when they requested flesh to eat. "[God] gave them their request; but sent leanness into their soul" (Psalm 106:15). A miracle was performed for them too (that of the quails), in order that they might have what they persisted in desiring. But there was only One who ever and always said, "Not my will, but thine, be done" (compare Psalm 21:4).

Manasseh quickly, it would seem, undid the work of his father's early reign.

> For he built again the high places which Hezekiah his father had broken down, and he reared up altars for Baalim, and

made groves, and worshipped all the host of heaven, and served them. Also he built altars [for idolatry] in the house of the LORD, whereof the LORD had said, In Jerusalem shall my name be for ever. And he built altars for all the host of heaven in the two courts of the house of the LORD. And he caused his children to pass through the fire in the valley of the son of Hinnom: also he observed times, and used enchantments, and used witchcraft, and dealt with a familiar spirit, and with wizards: he wrought much evil in the sight of the LORD, to provoke him to anger. And he set a carved image, the idol which he had made, in the house of God (2 Chronicles 33:3–7).

It is a terrible portrait to paint of any man; but of a king of Judah, and a son of Hezekiah the good, it seems almost incredible. It makes the heart almost sick, to read the list of his abominations. He "made Judah and the inhabitants of Jerusalem to err, and to do worse than the heathen, whom the LORD had destroyed before the children of Israel." It was the worst of all corruptions—the corruption of the best. The higher the fall, the deeper the plunge. Sadly, in the Corinthian church too there was such sin as was "not so much as named among the Gentiles" (1 Corinthians 5:1). Solomon wrote, "I was almost in all evil in the midst of the congregation and assembly" (Proverbs 5:14). Language like this may sound strange to some—strangely sad, indeed, that such things can be said of God's church. And what must the surrounding nations have thought of these annals of Judah—"worse than the heathen"? Of Manasseh and Judah it could then truly be said, as the apostle through the Spirit declared seven hundred years later, "The name of God is blasphemed among the Gentiles through you."

"And the LORD spake to Manasseh, and to his people: but they would not hearken." He spoke, as usual, through His prophets (2 Kings 21:10). This was their message:

> Because Manasseh king of Judah hath done these abominations, and hath done wickedly above all that the Amorites did [how terrible], which were before him, and hath made Judah also to sin with his idols: Therefore thus saith the LORD God of Israel, Behold, I am bringing such evil upon Jerusalem and Judah, that whosoever heareth of it, both his ears shall tingle. And I will stretch over Jerusalem the line of Samaria, and the plummet of the house of Ahab: and I will wipe Jerusalem as a man wipeth a dish, wiping it, and turning it upside down. And I will forsake the remnant of mine inheritance, and deliver them into the hand of their enemies; and they shall become a prey and a spoil to all their enemies; Because they have done that which was evil in my sight, and have provoked me to anger, since the day their fathers came forth out of Egypt, even unto this day (2 Kings 21:11–15).

It was an appalling, though absolutely just, indictment and should have brought the nation to repentance. Its threats, if nothing more, should have startled them from their sins. They knew the fate of Samaria—already fallen; and Jerusalem should receive like punishment. The house of Ahab had perished, and their kings would not escape a similar judgment. But the message was evidently lost on them; they proved themselves a more perverse people than the men of Nineveh who one hundred and fifty years before had repented at the preaching of Jonah.

What prophets God used at this time is not known. Possibly Isaiah was still alive, though very aged, and the tradition may be true that says he "was sawn asunder" with a wooden saw. Josephus does not mention this, though he does say that Manasseh "barbarously slew all the righteous men that were among the Hebrews. Nor would he spare the prophets, for he every day slew some of them, till Jerusalem was overflown

Manasseh

with blood" (*Antiquities* 10.3.1). "Moreover," said the inspired historian, "Manasseh shed innocent blood very much, till he had filled Jerusalem from one end to another; beside his sin wherewith he made Judah to sin, in doing that which was evil in the sight of the LORD" (2 Kings 21:16). Wicked as his grandfather Ahaz had been, he did not, so far as we know, redden his hands with blood like this human monster Manasseh. But the reaping came at last, though harvest time was late, perhaps because of the longsuffering patience of God. "Wherefore the LORD brought upon them the captains of the host of the king of Assyria, which took Manasseh among the thorns, and bound him with fetters, and carried him to Babylon" (2 Chronicles 33:11). They refused to hear the word, so they were compelled to feel the rod. As befitted this monster of evil, Manasseh was brought in chains to Babylon.

Scripture gives no hint as to the time of this event, but it appears from Assyrian monuments to have been somewhere about the middle of his reign. It was the old and often demonstrated law of retribution working itself out: the occasion of the sin becoming the instrument of its punishment. Hezekiah sinned in the "matter of the ambassadors" from Babylon, and it is to Babylon that his son Manasseh goes as a captive.

"And when he was in affliction, he besought the LORD his God, and humbled himself greatly before the God of his fathers, And prayed unto him: and he was entreated of him, and heard his supplication, and brought him again to Jerusalem into his kingdom. Then Manasseh knew that [Jehovah] he was God" (12–13). "He humbled himself greatly," as well he might, for his guilt indeed was very great. No doubt when he was in affliction he admitted the justice of his punishment. "I know, O LORD," he could say, "that thy judgments are right, and that thou in faithfulness hast afflicted me" (Psalm 119:75).

We have no details of Manasseh's sufferings in his Babylonian captivity. God takes no pleasure in the punishment of His people, and very tenderly covers with the veil of silence all that can be profitably kept back. He heard Manasseh's bitter cry of repentance and entreaty, and restored him to his kingdom. This was grace indeed—grace abounding.

On his return to Jerusalem he began to build and fortify, and put military commanders in all the fenced cities. But, what was better, "he took away the strange gods, and the idol out of the house of the LORD, and all the altars that he had built in the mount of the house of the LORD, and in Jerusalem, and cast them out of the city. And he repaired the altar of the LORD, and sacrificed thereon peace offerings and thank offerings, and commanded Judah to serve the LORD God of Israel" (2 Chronicles 33:15–16). He undertook to undo, as far as possible, his former works of wickedness. His name Manasseh means "forgetting"; and Josephus wrote: "When he was come to Jerusalem, he endeavored, if it were possible, to cast out of his memory those his former sins against God, of which he now repented, and to apply himself to a very religious life" (*Antiquities* 10.3.2). But the innocent lives that he had taken he could never restore, nor could he ever wholly undo the evil of his former course. So great had been his iniquity, and that of Judah with him, that God never forgave it nationally (2 Kings 23:26; 24:4; Jeremiah 15:4). *Personally,* through his confession and humiliation before God, Manasseh was forgiven. It is good to see the great change in his after life, and that he did not forget his indebtedness to God for His matchless grace to him, as his thank offerings on the restored altar indicate. He was the Old Testament chief of sinners, a type of the sinner in whom God shows forth all longsuffering, to any who would turn to Him in penitence and faith. Newton's lines well express the spirit of his grateful thoughts:

Amazing grace! how sweet the sound,
That saved a wretch like me!
I once was lost, but now am found,
Was blind, but now I see!

"And Manasseh slept with his fathers, and was buried in the garden of his own house, in the garden of Uzza: and Amon his son reigned in his stead" (2 Kings 21:18). His body found no place of rest among the kings, showing how the consequences of sin follow men even to the grave.

> Kings . . . on the throne; yea, he doth establish them for ever, and they are exalted. And if they be bound in fetters, and be holden in cords of affliction; Then he sheweth them their work, and their transgressions that they have exceeded. He openeth also their ear to discipline, and commandeth that they return from iniquity. If they obey and serve him, they shall spend their days in prosperity, and their years in pleasures. But if they obey not, they shall perish by the sword, and they shall die without knowledge (Job 36:7–12).

AMON

Training, or skilled
(2 Kings 21:19–26; 2 Chronicles 33:21–25)

Is it fit to say to a king, Thou art wicked? and to princes, Ye are ungodly?

Job 34:18

Amon was probably born after his father's return from Babylon.

Amon was twenty and two years old when he began to reign, and he reigned two years in Jerusalem. And his mother's name was Meshullemeth, the daughter of Haruz of Jotbah. And he did that which was evil in the sight of the LORD, as his father Manasseh did. And he walked in all the way that his father walked in, and served the idols that his father served, and worshipped them:

And he forsook the LORD God of his fathers, and walked not in the way of the LORD (2 Kings 21:19–22).

He must have had a godly training, as the expression, "he forsook the LORD," would seem to indicate that he had in his earlier days professed to worship Him. His mother's name, *Meshullemeth* ("reconciliation" or "to be safe"), might have reference to his having been born subsequently to her husband's reconciliation to the Lord, or his safe return from his Babylonian captivity. This would increase Amon's responsibility—having had such advantages—and consequently enhance his guilt. Her father's name, *Haruz* ("earnest") of *Jotbah* ("pleasantness"), leads to the supposition that Amon's mother, like his grandmother, must have been a good woman. But all good women do not always prove to be good mothers. It would be no strange or unusual thing if some of these Hebrew heirs apparent to the throne were permitted to do pretty much as they pleased, and in this way prepared to act the part of self-willed transgressors and rebels against God when the time came for them to take the kingdom. For "a child left to himself bringeth his mother to shame" (Proverbs 29:15).

There is not one bright spot in this king's character to relieve the darkness of his life's brief record. The chronicler wrote that he "humbled not himself before the LORD, as Manasseh his father had humbled himself; but Amon trespassed more and more" (or "multiplied trespass"). So odious did he make himself, even to the backslidden people, that they rid themselves of his unwelcome presence by the hands of assassins. "And his servants conspired against him, and slew him in his own house." His subjects must have been reduced to desperate straits when they would thus violate God's expressed prohibition—"Touch not mine anointed" (1 Chronicles 16:22). Jeremiah and Zephaniah must have been youths about this time, and the former's reluctance to take up the prophetic work to which he was called can well be understood when the true condition of affairs in Judah at that time is known. Both could see quite plainly what they might expect if faithful to their trust.

"But the people of the land slew all them that had conspired against king Amon; and the people of the land made Josiah his son king in his stead" (33:25). The center of light and privilege is not always the seat of righteousness and godly sincerity, but often the reverse is true. The unsophisticated citizens of the land are frequently more loyal and upright than the imperious citizens of the palace.

The record of the reign of Amon is most briefly told—in only sixteen verses. And well it should be so. There is enough for our admonition, after the lessons given in his father's history.

"And he was buried in his sepulchre in the garden of Uzza: and Josiah his son reigned in his stead." *Uzza* means "strength"; death, the strong one, overcame this king of Judah, whose name meant "trained," or "skilled." Indeed Amon was skilled in wickedness, and was assassinated in his twenty-fourth year.

"He passed away, and, lo, he was not: yea, I sought him, but he could not be found" (Psalm 37:36).

JOSIAH

Supported by Jehovah
(2 Kings 22–23; 2 Chronicles 34–35)

CONTEMPORARY PROPHET: Jeremiah

A wise king scattereth the wicked, and bringeth the wheel over them.

Proverbs 20:26

At last, after more than three hundred years, the prophecy of "the man of God out of Judah" is fulfilled: "Behold, a child shall be born unto the house of David, Josiah by name; and upon thee [the idol altar at Bethel] shall he offer the priests of the high places that burn incense upon thee, and men's bones shall be burnt upon thee" (1 Kings 13:2).

> Josiah was eight years old when he began to reign ... And he did that which was right in the sight of the LORD ... For in the eighth year of his reign, while he was yet young [sixteen], he began to seek after the God of David his father: and in the twelfth year he began to purge Judah and Jerusalem from the high places, and the groves, and the carved images, and the molten images. And they brake down the altars of Baalim in his presence; and the images [sun-pillars], that were on high above them, he cut down; and the groves, and the carved images, and the molten images, he brake in pieces, and made dust of them, and strowed it upon the graves of them that had sacrificed unto them. And he burnt the bones of the priests upon their altars, and cleansed Judah and Jerusalem (2 Chronicles 34:1–5).

"God's purposes will ripen fast," is true in a certain sense; yet in another sense, "The mills of God grind slow."

Scoffers long may have asked, "Where is the promise of this coming prince, this child of the house of David, named Josiah?" And as generation after generation passed, and no prince of that name appeared, even the righteous may have questioned in their minds and wondered if God had forgotten, or doubted if the prophecy were really true. Did *Jedidah* ("beloved") know of this prophecy when she named her first-born? or the child's grandmother, *Adaiah* ("Jah has adorned")? They were of the town of *Boscath,* a "swell" (of ground), and at last the time had come when he should rise of whom the prophet had spoken; and the prophecy was now fulfilled—as all God's word must be.

"And so did he in the cities of Manasseh, and Ephraim, and Simeon, even unto Naphtali, with their mattocks round about. And when he had broken down the altars and the groves, and had beaten the graven images into powder, and

Josiah

cut down all the idols throughout all the land of Israel, he returned to Jerusalem" (6–7). It took six years of labor to accomplish this; and "in the eighteenth year of his reign, when he had purged the land, and the house," he commissioned his officers of state to repair God's house. Levites were sent throughout the land to collect the money necessary for this work.

> And they put it in the hand of the workmen that had the oversight of the house of the LORD, and they gave it to the workmen that wrought in the house of the LORD, to repair and amend the house: even to the artificers and builders gave they it, to buy hewn stone, and timber for couplings [or joists], and to floor the houses which the kings of Judah had destroyed. And the men did the work faithfully (10–12).

Manasseh, though restored personally, had not the energy—or influence perhaps—to do this work. Everything must have been in a ruined state when the young Josiah began his work of restoration.

And now a great discovery was made. A hid treasure (long lost, no doubt) was found, better than of gold or rubies rare.

And when they brought out the money that was brought into the house of the Lord, Hilkiah the priest found a book of the law of the Lord given by Moses. And Hilkiah answered and said to Shaphan the scribe, I have found the book of the law in the house of the Lord. And Hilkiah delivered the book to Shaphan. And Shaphan carried the book to the king.

At first Shaphan said nothing of the new-found treasure. It may not have been a treasure in his eyes. Like many at the present time, he was more occupied with workmen and money than with God's book, which He has magnified, not merely above all Christian work or missionary enterprise (though these have their place), but "above all [His] name" (Psalm

138:2). Shaphan did not despise the book, but he had not yet, like many a modern scribe, realized the importance of that blessed volume. Then—after money, and overseers, and workmen, had all been mentioned—"then, Shaphan the scribe told the king, saying, Hilkiah the priest hath given me a book"—only *a* book! "And Shaphan read it before the king."

"And it came to pass, when the king had heard the words of the law, that he rent his clothes" (34:19). He then commanded the temple curators, and his servant Asaiah, "Go, inquire of the LORD for me, and for them that are left in Israel and in Judah, concerning the words of the book that is found: for great is the wrath of the LORD that is poured out upon us, because our fathers have not kept the word of the LORD, to do after all that is written in this book" (34:21). It was no doubt the Pentateuch—either the original, as written by Moses, or the temple copy (Deuteronomy 31:26) used in days gone by at the coronation of their kings (see Deuteronomy 17:18; 2 Chronicles 23:11). How long it had been lost is not known; probably since the beginning of Manasseh's reign at least.

"And Hilkiah, and they that the king had appointed, went to Huldah the prophetess, the wife of Shallum the son of Tikvath, the son of Hasrah, keeper of the wardrobe, (now she dwelt in Jerusalem in the college [or the second district];) and they spoke to her to that effect" (34:22). Why they did not inquire of Jeremiah, or Zephaniah (who were contemporary with Josiah—Jeremiah 1:3; Zephaniah 1:1), is uncertain. Anathoth, Jeremiah's birthplace, was only three miles from Jerusalem, and so within easy reach. Both these prophets however may have been too young at the time to be consulted as prophets by the nation (see Jeremiah 1:2).

Huldah's answer was a most impressive one. In wrath God remembers mercy; and like his great-grandfather Hezekiah, Josiah is comforted with the assurance that there would be a

Josiah

postponement of the impending judgments during his day because he, like Hezekiah, humbled himself. He at once gathered all the elders of the land together, and with them and the priests and Levites, "and all the people, great and small: and he [or, one] read in their ears all the words of the book of the covenant that was found in the house of the LORD."

"And the king stood by a pillar, and made a covenant before [Jehovah], to walk after [Jehovah], and to keep his commandments and his testimonies and his statutes with all [his] heart and with all [his] soul, to perform the words of this covenant that were written in this book. And all the people stood to the covenant" (2 Kings 23:3). On the young king's part this was all real, no doubt, but one has only to read the earlier part of Jeremiah's prophecy to see how hypocritical it was with the mass of the people (see Jeremiah 3:10). They had enthusiastically entered into covenants with the Lord before, and the outcome was always the same—breakdown, and wider departure from God than ever before.

The work of reformation is then extended: "And Josiah took away all the abominations out of all the countries that pertained to the children of Israel, and made all that were present in Israel to serve, even to serve the LORD their God. And all his days they departed not from following the LORD, the God of their fathers" (2 Chronicles 34:33).

> Moreover the altar that was at Bethel, and the high place which Jeroboam the son of Nebat, who made Israel to sin, had made, both that altar and the high place he brake down ... And as Josiah turned himself, he spied the sepulchres that were there in the mount, and sent, and took the bones out of the sepulchres, and burned them upon the altar, and polluted it, according to the word of the LORD which the man of God proclaimed, who proclaimed these words [see 1 Kings 13:2].

KINGS OF JUDAH

Then he said, What title is that that I see? And the men of the city told him, It is the sepulchre of the man of God which came from Judah, and proclaimed these things that thou hast done against the altar of Bethel. And he said, Let him alone; let no man move his bones. So they let his bones alone, with the bones of the prophet that came out of Samaria (2 Kings 23:15–18).

It is not certain if this remarkable incident occurred before or after the finding of the copy of the law in the temple (see Author's Introduction). It proves however that after the lapse of at least three centuries the prophecy of the Judean prophet was still fresh in the minds of men. God not only lets none of His words fall to the ground, but takes care also that in some way or other they are preserved in the memories of those concerned in them. No doubt the inscription on the tomb of the man of God would help to keep the occurrence from being forgotten. How awed and encouraged Josiah the king must have felt, to know that he had been named and appointed by God, so many generations before, for the work he was doing. How it would tend to impress on him the force and meaning of such scriptures as Psalm 139. And witnessing how literally the prophecy of the man of God was fulfilled, he and all his people, would be convinced that the prophecies of Huldah and Jeremiah against themselves would in like manner be exactly fulfilled.

Moved, no doubt, by what was written in the recovered book of the law regarding the passover, Josiah began proceedings to commemorate this forgotten feast in Jerusalem. Careful preparations were made that everything might be done according to the written word of God. It was in the eighteenth year of his reign, so was probably celebrated immediately after the completion of the temple repairs and the

Josiah

finding of the book (compare 2 Chronicles 34:8 and 35:19).

> And he set the priests in their charges, and encouraged them to the service of the house of the LORD. And said unto the Levites that taught all Israel, which were holy unto the LORD, Put the holy ark in the house which Solomon the son of David king of Israel did build, it shall not be a burden upon your shoulders: serve now the LORD your God and His people Israel. And prepare yourselves by the houses of your fathers, after your courses, according to the writing of David king of Israel, and according to the writing of Solomon his son (2 Chronicles 35:2–4).

It was all to be done *according to what was written.* Josiah evidently took great care as to this, and so became a beautiful example for all who long to please and follow the Lord, declining "neither to the right hand nor to the left," like this godly king. Some in the kingdom might think him too much bound to the letter of these writings, but he would have God's approval, which was quite enough. No one can say where the willful departure of a hair's breadth may not eventually lead. The safety of all is to keep as far away from the edge of the precipice as possible. "Then shall I not be ashamed, when I have respect unto all thy commandments" (Psalm 119:6).

Josiah told the Levites to put the ark in its proper place in the temple, and not bear it any longer on their shoulders. This is the last historical reference to the ark in Scripture. It would almost appear, from Jeremiah 3:16, that it had been made an object of ostentatious display and was possibly carried by the Levites in procession through the streets of Jerusalem. It is never after heard of, and probably destroyed when the temple was burned by the Chaldees (2 Chronicles 36:19).

KINGS OF JUDAH

The king further commanded the Levites: "Kill the passover, and sanctify yourselves, and prepare your brethren, that they may do *according to the Word of the* LORD *by the hand of Moses*" (italics added). And such a passover it was! "There was no passover like to that kept in Israel from the days of Samuel the prophet; neither did all the kings of Israel keep such a passover as Josiah kept, and the priests, and the Levites, and all Judah and Israel that were present, and the inhabitants of Jerusalem" (35:18). It even exceeded the great passover under Hezekiah, which had not been equaled since "the time of Solomon son of David king of Israel" (2 Chronicles 30:26). Josiah's Passover surpassed that of all the kings, and found its equal only in that of the prophet Samuel.

And now comes the closing act in this stirring drama of Josiah's life.

> After all this, when Josiah had prepared the temple, Necho king of Egypt came up to fight against Charchemish by Euphrates: and Josiah went out against him. But he sent ambassadors to him, saying, What have I to do with thee, thou king of Judah? I come not against thee this day, but against the house wherewith I have war: for God commanded me to make haste: forbear thee from meddling with God, who is with me, that he destroy thee not (35:20–21).

Josiah was given a fair warning and he should certainly have heeded it. Necho came against Assyria, and had no quarrel with Josiah. He was a man of enterprise and energy. It was he who attempted to connect the Red Sea with the Nile by a canal. Phoenician navigators, under his patronage, circumnavigated the continent of Africa. He came by sea on this expedition, and landed at Accho. So he was not even on Josiah's territory when that king marched his forces against him.

Josiah

Nevertheless Josiah would not turn his face from him, but disguised himself, that he might fight with him, and hearkened not unto the words of Necho from the mouth of God, and came to fight in the valley of Megiddo. And the archers shot at king Josiah; and the king said to his servants, Have me away; for I am sore wounded. His servants therefore took him out of that chariot, and put him in the second chariot that he had; and they brought him to Jerusalem, and he died, and was buried in one of the sepulchres of his fathers (35:22–24).

"Why shouldest thou meddle to thy hurt, that thou shouldest fall?" said the king of Israel to Amaziah, Josiah's ancestor, years before (2 Kings 14:10). Josiah should also have been familiar with the proverb that had been copied by the men of Hezekiah, "He that passeth by, and meddleth with strife belonging not to him, is like one that taketh a dog by the ears" (Proverbs 26:17). And another: "It is an honour for a man to cease from strife: but every fool will be meddling" (Proverbs 20:3). It was not an act of faith, else why disguise himself? There is no record of any prayer before the battle, as in the case of so many of his godly ancestors; and this rash act of Josiah seems unaccountable. He may have suspected that Necho had some ulterior design on his kingdom. But as the king of Egypt strongly disclaimed any such intention, Josiah's unprovoked attack on him was wholly unjustified. And God, who is the God of peace and righteousness, would not preserve him, as he had Jehoshaphat. We may look at Josiah's early end in another way: The people were utterly unworthy of such a godly ruler, and their wickedness, in spite of external reformation, called loudly for judgment, so the righteous was taken away from the evil to come. Viewed from this standpoint, it was a mercy to the man himself; but to the nation at that time, it seemed a dire calamity.

KINGS OF JUDAH

They evidently realized this, for we read, "All Judah and Jerusalem mourned for Josiah. And Jeremiah lamented for Josiah: and all the singing men and the singing women spake of Josiah in their lamentations to this day, and made them an ordinance in Israel: and, behold, they are written in the lamentations." These "lamentations" must not be confused with Jeremiah's Lamentations, written after Jerusalem's fall (compare Jeremiah 22:10; Zechariah 12:11).

Josiah was the last good king to sit on the throne of David, "till He come whose right it is." And he was the last whose body found a resting place among the kings, "the sepulchres of his fathers."

The memory of this just and energetic king is blessed. When only twenty years of age he began the herculean task of cleansing his kingdom of its abominations (2 Kings 23:4–14). There were vessels used in idolatrous worship to be removed from the temple; there were "idolatrous priests whom the kings of Judah had ordained," to be "put down"—them that burned incense to "Baal, to the sun, and to the moon, and to the planets." "And he brake down the houses of the sodomites [men consecrated to vile purposes], that were by the house of the LORD, where the women [also consecrated to heathen deities] wove hangings [tents] for the groves." Joshua the governor of the city had high places at the entrance of his gate. Josiah fearlessly destroyed them. He took away the "horses that the kings of Judah had given to the sun, at the entering in of the house of the Lord, by the chamber of Nathan-melech the chamberlain . . . and burned the chariots of the sun with fire. And the altars that were on the top [or roof] of the upper chamber of Ahaz, which the kings of Judah had made, and the altars which Manasseh had made in the two courts of the house of the LORD, did the king beat down" (or shattered). He seems to have had few sympathizers or supporters in his

Josiah

reforms, and superintended some of the work personally (see 2 Kings 23:16). He could not be blamed if the mass of the people were hypocritical and unreal (see Zephaniah 1:5). Genuine repentance is not brought about by a king's command, but he did all that lay in his power, and did not permit a single visible vestige of idolatry to remain in his realm. It is significant that when this last righteous king of Judah died, the whole land was outwardly cleansed of its abominations. And when his work was done, God called him home, though an Egyptian arrow was His messenger. "And like unto him was there no king before him, that turned to the LORD with all his heart, and with all his soul, and with all his might, according to all the law of Moses; neither after him arose there any like him" (2 Kings 23:25).

JEHOAHAZ
(or Shallum)

Jehovah-seized
(2 Kings 23:30–34; 2 Chronicles 36:1–4)

CONTEMPORARY PROPHETS: Jeremiah, Habakkuk, Zephaniah

The kings of the earth, and all the inhabitants of the world, would not have believed that the adversary and the enemy should have entered into the gates of Jerusalem.

Lamentations 4:12

The regular succession to the throne of Judah ceased with the lamented Josiah. Jehoahaz was not the eldest son of the late king. Johanan and Jehoiakim were both older than he. In Jeremiah 22:11 he is called, significantly, *Shallum* ("to whom it is requited"), and by this name he is registered in the royal Judean genealogy (1 Chronicles 3:15). He was made king by popular choice: it was the preference of the multitude, not the appointment of God. "And his mother's name was Hamutal ["delight"], the daughter of Jeremiah of Libnah. And he did that which was evil in the sight of the LORD, according to all that his fathers had done." He and Zedekiah, the last of Judah's nineteen kings, were born of the same mother (2 Kings 24:18). He was about nine years older than his brother Zedekiah, though in 1 Chronicles 3:15 his name is placed last, probably because of his much shorter reign.

He is likened in Ezekiel 19:1–4 to "a young lion, and it learned to catch the prey; it devoured men." This is the only hint given us as to the character of his sin. Josephus said of him that he was "an impious man, and impure in his course of life" (*Antiquities* 10.5.2). He was probably guilty of deeds of violence. His name is omitted from among those of our Lord's ancestors in Matthew 1. Necho, it is said, made Jehoahaz' half brother Eliakim "king in the room of Josiah his father," which may imply that God did not recognize Jehoahaz, the people's choice, as being in a true sense the successor.

"And the king of Egypt put him down at Jerusalem, and condemned the land in a hundred talents of silver and a talent of gold" (2 Chronicles 36:3). It is elsewhere stated that he was taken to Riblah in the land of Hamath and bound, which in no wise contradicts what is quoted above. History informs us that after his victory at Megiddo, Necho intended to march to the Euphrates. But hearing of Jehoahaz' elevation to the throne by popular acclamation, he sent a division of his army to Jerusalem, which deposed him and brought him captive to Riblah, where Necho and his chief forces were. This he did, it is said, because he believed Jehoahaz leaned toward an alliance with Assyria against him.

"And the king of Egypt made Eliakim his brother king over Judah and Jerusalem, and turned his name to Jehoiakim.

Jehoahaz

And Necho took Jehoahaz his brother, and carried him to Egypt." He never returned from Egypt. Jehoahaz ("Jehovah-seized") had seized the throne that was not his by right, and in turn he was seized by Necho, God's instrument. He was carried to a land of exile, there to find a grave far from the sepulchres of his fathers.

He was anointed at his coronation, but no extraordinary ceremony could make up for his defective title to the crown (2 Kings 23:30). Men have similar thoughts today. They feel they have no real title to a throne in Heaven with Christ, so they increase forms and elaborate ceremonies. Hence the rapid growth of ritualism. "And the end is not yet."

JEHOIAKIM

Whom Jehovah will raise
(2 Kings 23:34–24:6; 2 Chronicles 36:5–8)

CONTEMPORARY PROPHETS: Jeremiah, Zephaniah, Ezekiel

His confidence shall be rooted out of his tabernacle, and it shall bring him to the king of terrors.

Job 18:41

Jehoiakim was a most unlovely character—treacherous, vengeful, and blood-thirsty. He was several years Jehoahaz' senior, and was not born of the same mother. "And his mother's name was Zebudah ['gainfulness'], the daughter of Pedaiah of Ramah." The mother's name was a good prediction of her son's behavior. He taxed the land to get the money demanded by Pharaoh: "he exacted the silver and the gold of the people of the land, of every one according to his taxation, to give unto Pharaoh-Necho." Having been slighted by the people in their choice of his younger half brother, he would make no effort to ease the people's burdens, but rather increase them. He was in no way under obligations to them; and having behind him the power of Egypt, he had little to fear from them (see 2 Kings 23:34–35).

His wickedness is depicted figuratively in Ezekiel 19:5–7. He too, like his deposed predecessor, "became a young lion, and learned to catch the prey, and devoured men. And he knew their desolate palaces, and he laid waste their cities; and the land was desolate, and the fullness thereof, by the noise of his roaring." His violence and rapacity are graphically represented here.

In the fifth year of his reign a fast was proclaimed among his subjects (the king seems to have had no part in it), and Baruch, Jeremiah's assistant, read in the ears of all the people the message of God to them from a book. Informants told the king what was being done, and he ordered the book brought and read before him.

> Now the king sat in the winterhouse in the ninth month: and there was a fire on the hearth burning before him. And it came to pass, that when Jehudi had read three or four leaves, he cut it with the penknife [Hebrew: "scribe's knife"], and cast it into the fire that was on the hearth, until all the roll was consumed in the fire that was on the hearth. Yet they were not afraid, nor rent their garments, neither the king, nor any of his servants that heard all these words (Jeremiah 36:22–24).

It was an act of daring impiety, especially for a Jew who was taught to look upon all sacred writing with greatest reverence. But Jehoiakim was fast hardening himself past all feeling, and no qualms of conscience are perceptible over his sacrilegious act. Jeremiah sent him a personal and verbal message, more awful than any king ever heard.

> And thou shalt say to Jehoiakim king of Judah, Thus saith the Lord; Thou hast burned this roll, saying, Why hast thou written therein, saying, The king of Babylon shall certainly come and destroy this land, and shall cause to cease from thence man and beast? Therefore thus saith the LORD of Jehoiakim king of Judah; He shall have none to sit upon the throne of David: and his dead body shall be cast out in the day to the heat, and in the night to the frost. And I will punish him and his seed and his servants for their iniquity (29–31).

He also attempted to put Urijah the prophet to death because he prophesied against Jerusalem and the land. The prophet fled to Egypt, but Jehoiakim sent and fetched him, and "slew him with the sword, and cast his dead body into the graves of the common people" (Jeremiah 26:23). His bitter hatred of God and His truth vented itself even on the body of His slaughtered servant, denying it the right of burial among the sepulchers of the prophets. In just retribution God repaid him in kind for his murder and insult. "Therefore thus saith the LORD concerning Jehoiakim the son of Josiah king of Judah: They shall not lament for him, saying, Ah my brother! or, Ah sister! [as in family mourning] they shall not lament for him, saying, Ah lord! or, Ah his glory! [public mourning] He shall be buried with the burial of an ass, drawn and cast forth beyond the gates of Jerusalem" (Jeremiah 22:18–19). And so it happened to him: Nebuchadnezzar defeated and drove out of Asia Jehoiakim's master, Necho (see 2 Kings 24:7). "In his days Nebuchadnezzar king of Babylon came up, and Jehoiakim became his servant three years: then he turned and rebelled against him" (2 Kings 24:1). And though Nebuchadnezzar could not immediately punish him, his punishment came from another quarter. "The LORD sent against him bands of the Chaldees, and bands of the Syrians, and bands of the Moabites, and bands of the children of Ammon, and sent them against Judah to destroy it, according to the word of the LORD, which he spake by his servants the prophets."

Scripture (historically) is silent regarding his end. Second Chronicles 36:6 states that Nebuchadnezzar "bound him in fetters, to carry him to Babylon." It does not say he *was* taken there. He may have been released after promising subjection to his conqueror. But even if it could be proven that he was actually carried to Babylon, it would in no wise contradict what is recorded in 2 Kings 24:6 ("So Jehoiakim slept with his fathers"). He might easily have returned to Jerusalem, as other Jewish captives at a later date did. And though there is no historical record in Scripture concerning his death, this does not prove that the prophecies of Jeremiah concerning his end were not fulfilled to the letter. We do not really need the history of it, for prophecy in Scripture is only prewritten history—the advance sheets, we might say. It is enough to know what God had foretold concerning it; the fulfillment is certain. Josephus stated that Nebuchadnezzar finally came and slew Jehoiakim, "whom he commanded to be thrown before the walls, without any burial" (*Antiquities* 10.6.3). "So Jehoiakim slept with his fathers" simply expresses his death; it is a distinct expression in Scripture from "buried with his fathers," as a comparison of 2 Kings 15:38 and 16:20 will readily show. So the king who denied the prophet's body honorable burial was himself "*buried* with the burial of an ass." He mutilated and burnt God's book, and his body was in turn torn and burnt unburied in the scorching sun.

His wicked life was a sad contrast to that of his righteous

Jehoiakim

father. Jeremiah asked, "Did not thy father eat and drink [lived plainly], and do judgment and justice, and then it was well with him? He judged the cause of the poor and needy; then it was well with him: was not this to know me? saith the LORD" (Jeremiah 22:15–16). Necho changed his name, but could not change his nature.

"Now the rest of the acts of Jehoiakim, and his abominations which he did, and that which was found in him, behold, they are written in the book of the kings of Israel and Judah: and Jehoiachin his son reigned in his stead" (2 Chronicles 36:8).

His name, like that of his brother, is omitted from the royal genealogy of Matthew 1. "His uncleanness and iniquity" are mentioned in the Apocrypha (1 Esdras 1:42). During his reign (when Nebuchadnezzar took the kingdom) the times of the Gentiles began. And until they are fulfilled, Jerusalem "shall be trodden under foot," even as it is this day.

JEHOIACHIN

Jehovah will establish
(2 Kings 24:8–17; 25:27–30; 2 Chronicles 36:9–10)

CONTEMPORARY PROPHETS: Jeremiah, Zephaniah, Ezekiel

He looseth the bond of kings, and girdeth their loins with a girdle.
Job 12:18

Jehoiachin was eighteen years old when he began to reign, and he reigned in Jerusalem three months. And his mother's name was Nehushta, the daughter of Elnathan of Jerusalem. And he did that which was evil in the sight of the LORD, according to all that his father had done" (2 Kings 24:8–9). Various English versions of 2 Chronicles 36:9, as well as the Septuagint and Vulgate, make him eight years old at the beginning of his reign, instead of eighteen. But some Hebrew manuscripts, Syriac, and Arabic, read "eighteen" in Chronicles; so *eight* must be an error of transcription. All the internal evidence is in favor of eighteen.

His character was no different from that of his two predecessors. It is the same sad, unvarying record: "He did that which was evil." How the godly must have longed for that King mentioned by Isaiah, who would reign in righteousness! They little knew or even suspected, perhaps, all that their nation would have to suffer, and the long, weary centuries—in fact, millennia—that would have to wear themselves away before that day of righteousness and peace would come. But there was something about even this wicked king that could give them hope—his name, "Jehovah will establish." They might not know the time; but they were assured of the fact. And so they could with patience wait for it.

Nehushta, his mother's name, means "copper." It refers to anything of copper, whether a copper coin, or a copper mirror or *fetters:* and both she and her son, with all his family and retinue, were carried captive to Babylon.

> And Nebuchadnezzar king of Babylon came against the city, and his servants did besiege it. And Jehoiachin the king of Judah went out to the king of Babylon, he, and his mother, and his servants, and his princes, and his officers: and the king of Babylon took him in the eighth year of his [Nebuchadnezzar's] reign. And he carried out thence all the treasures of the house of the LORD, and the treasures of the king's house, and cut in pieces all the vessels of gold which Solomon king of Israel had made in the temple of the LORD, as the LORD had said. And he carried away all Jerusalem, and all the princes, and all the mighty men of valour, even ten thousand captives, and all the craftsmen and smiths: none remained, save the poorest sort of the people of the land. And he carried away Jehoiachin

Jehoiachin

to Babylon, and the king's mother, and the king's wives" [*wives,* confirming his age as eighteen not eight], and his officers, and the mighty of the land, those carried he into captivity from Jerusalem to Babylon (2 Kings 24:11–15).

This was all "as the LORD said," through His prophet Jeremiah (Jeremiah 20:5). Heaven and earth will pass away and perish, but not one word of God.

The temple was despoiled of its remaining treasures. A few years before, the king of Babylon had carried away the solid and smaller vessels (2 Chronicles 36:7). On this occasion he (literal translation) "cut the gold off" the larger plated vessels—the ark, the altar of incense, the showbread table, etc. There is no contradiction here, or anywhere in Scripture, for "the Scripture cannot be broken." The king's mother would be the queen mother mentioned in Jeremiah 13:18.

The Babylonian captivity dates from Jehoiachin's reign. He never returned from his captivity. There he spent thirty-six years in prison until the death of Nebuchadnezzar in his eighty-third or eighty-fourth year, after a reign of forty-three years. His son Evil-merodach succeeded him on the throne. This son had once been himself shut up in prison by his father, where he probably made the acquaintance of the royal Hebrew captive. He was not like the ungrateful butler who when released from prison forgot Joseph; he remembered his old prison companion.

> And it came to pass in the seven and thirtieth year of the captivity of Jehoiachin king of Judah, in the twelfth month, in the five and twentieth day of the month, that Evil-merodach king of Babylon in the first year of his reign lifted up the head of Jehoiachin king of Judah, and brought him forth out of prison, and spake kindly unto him, and set his throne above the

throne of the kings that were with him in Babylon; and changed his prison garments: and he did continually eat bread before him all the days of his life. And for his diet there was a continual diet given him of the king of Babylon, every day a portion until the day of his death, all the days of his life (Jeremiah 52:31–34).

He was not the first king of David's house to be held a prisoner in Babylon. Some time before, his father's great-grandfather, Manasseh, was brought a prisoner, and there in his affliction he sought and found the Lord. Whether Jehoiachin ever did so, we cannot say. His name (as *Jechonias*) is the last of the kings of Judah, mentioned in the list of Matthew 1. The next is "Jesus who is called Christ," anointed King, not of Israel or the Jews only, but of the nations also (Revelation 15:3).

Jeremiah said of Jehoiakim, (Jehoiachin's father) "He shall have none to sit upon the throne of David" (Jeremiah 36:30). The word sit here means to "firmly sit" or "dwell," and Jehoiachin's short three-month reign was surely not that. And Zedekiah, Jehoiachin's successor, was Jehoiakim's brother, not his son.

Though, like his father, "he did evil in the sight of the LORD," Jehoiachin appears to have been a favorite with the populace. Jeremiah ironically inquired "Is this man Coniah a despised broken idol [or, vase]?" (In 1 Chronicles 3:17 Jehoiachin is called *Jeconiah,* of which *Coniah* is an abbreviation.) But he immediately added, "Is he a vessel wherein is no pleasure?"—which is really what he was in God's eyes. "Wherefore are they cast out, he and his seed, and are cast into a land which they knew not? O earth, earth, earth, hear the word of the LORD: Thus saith the LORD, Write ye this man childless, a man that shall not prosper in his days: for no man of his seed shall prosper, sitting upon the throne of David, and ruling any more in Judah" (Jeremiah 22:28–30). *Childless* here does not mean without descendants (for the prophecy itself mentions "his seed") but "no direct lineal heir to the throne" (Fausset). Matthew 1:12 shows conclusively that he had descendants ("Jechonias begat Salathiel"), as does also 1 Chronicles 3:17 ("The sons of Jeconiah; Assir," etc.). The prophecy of Jeremiah probably refers to his uncle's succeeding him to the throne instead of his son Assir—his firstborn probably; or it may have been a prophecy of Assir's premature death. This may be why Assir is not mentioned in the genealogy in Matthew. Anyway, God made no mistake. He speaks, and it is done; He commands, and it stands fast. "And the word of our God shall stand forever."

ZEDEKIAH

Righteousness of Jehovah
(2 Kings 24:17–25:21; 2 Chronicles 36:11–21)

CONTEMPORARY PROPHETS: Jeremiah, Ezekiel, Daniel, Obadiah

Her king and her princes are among the Gentiles: the law is no more: her prophets also find no vision from the Lord.
Lamentations 2:9

*A*nd the king of Babylon made Mattaniah his father's brother king in his [Jehoiachin's] stead, and changed his name to Zedekiah. Zedekiah was twenty and one years old when he began to reign, and he reigned eleven years in Jerusalem" (2 Kings 24:17–18).

Zedekiah was Josiah's youngest son, and full brother of Jehoahaz. He was, at his father's death, only ten years old.

Nebuchadnezzar changed his name (as a token of his vassalage) but did not give him the name of some heathen deity, as in the case of Daniel and the three Hebrew children. He "had made him swear by God," and his new name—*Zedekiah* meaning "Righteousness of Jehovah"—may have been given him to remind him of his oath (2 Chronicles 36:13). Or the name may have had some connection, even in the heathen king's mind, with Jehovah's righteousness in taking from this wicked people (called by His name) their political independence, and subjecting them to his dominion.

"Zedekiah rebelled against the king of Babylon" (2 Kings 24:20). He had no real faith in Jehovah, Israel's covenant-keeping God, and therefore did not hesitate to break his covenant with Nebuchadnezzar. But how dearly he paid for this violation of his oath! "And it came to pass, in the ninth year of his reign...that Nebuchadnezzar king of Babylon came, he, and all his host, against Jerusalem...and the city was besieged unto the eleventh year of king Zedekiah" (2 Kings 25:1–2).

The occasion of this rebellion was Zedekiah's hope of assistance from the king of Egypt (see Ezekiel 17:11–21). He also vainly attempted to form an alliance with the surrounding nations, for the purpose of ridding himself, and them, of the yoke of the Babylonian king (see Jeremiah 27:1–11. Various ancient manuscripts have the name *Zedekiah* for *Jehoiakim* in 27:1. Compare with verses 3 and 12 and 28:1). Pharaoh-hophra attempted to relieve Zedekiah during the siege, but was driven back into Egypt by Nebuchadnezzar's army, who then returned and reoccupied Jerusalem (see Jeremiah 37:5–10). It was a terrible siege, lasting eighteen months; famine and pestilence prevailed. Mothers boiled and ate their own children (Lamentations 4:10). According to Josephus, at midnight the Chaldees gained entrance into the city, and the fugitive king was captured. He and his sons were brought to Nebuchadnezzar at Riblah, "on the high road between Palestine and Babylon, where the Babylonian kings remained in directing the operations of their armies in Palestine and Phenicia" (Fausset).

Here his terrible punishment was meted out to him for his deceit in violating his solemn compact with his master. After seeing his own children slain before him, his own eyes were dug out of their sockets, and he was bound "with double chains of bronze" (2 Kings 25:7, literal translation), and led off to Babylon. So the two seemingly contradictory prophecies of Jeremiah (32:4) and Ezekiel (12:13) were literally fulfilled. At Babylon he was cast into prison "till the day of his death" (Jeremiah 52:11). "Until I visit him" (Jeremiah 32:5) might imply that he was finally set at liberty, but "till the day of his death" precludes any such interpretation. It is more agreeable to take the expression to mean that God in mercy would visit him with repentance and a true knowledge of Himself as He did to Manasseh before him. How often God has used the stern hand of his government to break down the pride and rebellion of the heart, and through such "visitation" bring to the penitent soul the truest of all liberty—deliverance from the bondage of sin. So would his soul be set free, though his body remain in bondage. Adapting Richard Lovelace's poem, we could say:

> *Stone walls do not a prison make,*
> *Nor iron bars a cage,*
>
> . . . .
>
> *If I have freedom in [God's] love,*
> *And in my soul am free.*

Josephus said Nebuchadnezzar "kept Zedekiah in prison until he died; and then buried him magnificently." This agrees with Jeremiah 34:5; "Thou shalt die in peace: and with the burnings of thy fathers, the former kings which were before thee."

Zedekiah has been justly characterized as weak, vacillating, and treacherous. His weakness and subserviency to his princes mark him as a man wholly unfit to wear a crown, or sit on a throne: "Behold he [Jeremiah] is in your hand," he said to them, "for the king is not he that can do anything against you" (Jeremiah 38:5). He was hypocritical also. He feigned a desire for the prophet's prayers, saying, "Pray now unto the LORD our God for us" (Jeremiah 37:3). He pretended too, at times, to have confidence in the prophecies of Jeremiah ("Inquire, I pray thee, of the LORD for us," Jeremiah 21:2), which when delivered, he refused to heed or believe. "He did that which was evil in the sight of the LORD his God, and humbled not himself before Jeremiah the prophet speaking from the mouth of the LORD" (2 Chronicles 36:12). He was not so openly wicked as his three predecessors perhaps, and not willingly given to persecution. This is probably why Josephus, judging after the standards of men, wrote of "his gentle and righteous disposition." But the Lord sees not as man sees, neither are His thoughts man's thoughts. He said, "He stiffened his neck, and hardened his heart from turning unto the LORD God of Israel." So God took him away in His anger.

The temple was burned to the ground, and only a miserable remnant of the nation was left in the land: "The captain of the guard left of the poor of the land to be vinedressers, and husbandmen" (2 Kings 25:12). Rebellion arose even among these, and for fear of the Chaldees they fled to the land of Egypt, only to miserably perish there, as Jeremiah had faithfully and tearfully warned them.

Zedekiah

For seventy years the land lay desolate, after which a remnant was permitted to return. Six hundred years later wise men came from that very land of the East, inquiring where they might find Him that was "born King of the Jews."

Until that day the godly remnant of His heritage could only pray, in the words of David—the type of that coming King—"Oh let the wickedness of the wicked come to an end; but establish the just" (Psalm 7:9).

"Even so, come, LORD JESUS"!

BIBLIOGRAPHY

The author gratefully acknowledges the help of the following sources:

Darby, John Nelson. *Translation of the Old Testament.*

Fausset, Andrew Robert. *Bible Cyclopedia.*

Josephus, Flavius. *The Works of Josephus,* translated by William Whiston. Reprints available from the following publishers: Baker Book House; Hendrickson Publishers; Kregel Publications.

Strong, James. *Exhaustive Concordance of the Bible.* New York: Abingdon Press, 1890.

OTHER READING:

Thiele, E. R. *The Mysterious Numbers of the Hebrew Kings*

THE ECS CLASSIC SERIES

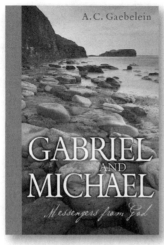

Gabriel and Michael

Kings of Israel

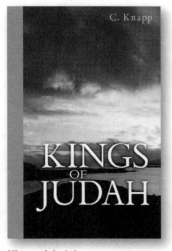

Kings of Judah

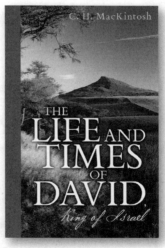

**The Life and Times
of David King of Israel**

YOU MAY ORDER BY PHONE AT:
1-888-338-7809

OR ONLINE AT:
www.ecsministries.org

THE ECS FOUNDATION SERIES

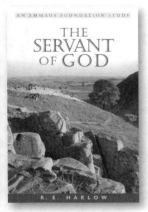
The Servant of God

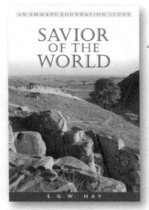
Savior of the World

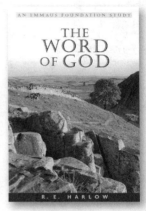
The Word of God

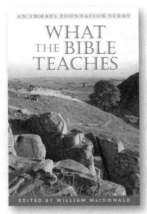
What the Bible Teaches

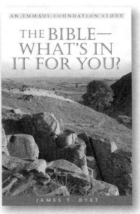
**The Bible—
What's in it For You?**

YOU MAY ORDER BY PHONE AT:
1-888-338-7809

OR ONLINE AT:
www.ecsministries.org

A DEVOTIONAL COMMENTARY

**Genesis
From Creation
to a Nation**

YOU MAY ORDER BY PHONE AT:
1-888-338-7809

OR ONLINE AT:
www.ecsministries.org